Faculty Incivility

Faculty Incivility

The Rise of the Academic Bully Culture and What to Do About It

Darla J. Twale
Barbara M. De Luca

JOSSEY-BASS
A Wiley Imprint
www.josseybass.com

Published by Jossey-Bass
A Wiley Imprint
989 Market Street, San Francisco, CA 94103-1741—www.josseybass.com

Jossey-Bass books and products are available through most bookstores. To contact Jossey-Bass directly call our Customer Care Department within the U.S. at 800-956-7739, outside the U.S. at 317-572-3986, or fax 317-572-4002.

Jossey-Bass also publishes its books in a variety of electronic formats. Some content that appears in print may not be available in electronic books.

Library of Congress Cataloging-in-Publication Data

Twale, Darla J. (Darla Jean)
  Faculty incivility : the rise of the academic bully culture and what to do about it / Darla J. Twale, Barbara M. De Luca.—1st ed.
      p. cm.
  Includes bibliographical references and index.
  ISBN 978-0-470-19766-0 (cloth)
   1. Universities and colleges—Faculty—Attitudes. 2. Bullying in the workplace.
3. Courtesy in the workplace. 4. Academic etiquette. I. Luca, Barbara M. De. II. Title.
  LB2331.7.T93 2008
  378.1'2—dc22

                                                                              2007040904

Printed in the United States of America
FIRST EDITION
HB Printing   10 9 8 7 6 5 4 3 2

Contents

Part III: Addressing Faculty Incivility and the Academic Bully Culture

To my mother, LaVerne, and my aunts, Hazel and Leona, whose back porch conversations alerted me to bullying in the workplace long before I took my first job. D.J.T.

To my mother and father, who taught me how to handle bullies, and to my daughter, to whom I hope I have passed on their wisdom. B.M.D.

Preface

L ately it seems that people in academe have become less civil
to one another. If you are a faculty member in academe
or a graduate student preparing for the profession, you may have
encountered instances of incivility, bullying, or mobbing by another
peer, a student, a committee, or an administrator. While bullying
tends to be done more one on one, mobbing implies that a group of
people are uncivil to one or more persons. You probably dismissed
the behavior the first time and perhaps the second, but when you
noticed a pattern developing that the behavior affected your work,
you knew it was more than just a trend in society. It was incivility.
It was an indication that perhaps the makings of a bully culture had
begun to manifest itself in your department, college, or institution.
Now what?

This book will help you deal with this situation: the actors,
the victims, and the possible causes of incivility. Linking the
problem to both internal and external sources is necessary to frame
a conceptual model and extend the work of others who have
begun writing on the subject of workplace aggression. Although
the research of these authors is outside academe and outside the
United States, there is no reason to believe that academe is exempt
from the problems and issues surrounding incivility, bullying, and
mobbing in the workplace. Our goal here is to uncover the personal,
social, cultural, organizational, and structural reasons that faculty

incivility may have led to the development of an academic bully culture. We begin with the popular press.

When asked by the *Chronicle of Higher Education* ("Pressing legal issues," 2004) for an opinion on pressing higher education issues, six of ten legal experts alluded to the issues we mention in this book as contributing to faculty incivility and the likelihood of a rising academic bully culture. For instance, Christine Helwich of the California State University system mentioned changes in current faculty demographics. Would this affect higher education in negative ways? Martin Mickelson, a partner in the law firm of Hogan and Harsten in Washington, D.C., addressed worker rights and that the paucity of law on academic freedom could raise concerns within the academic culture. Could one concern be faculty incivility? Brown University counsel Beverly Leadbetter and University of Houston law professor Michael Olivas each noted that the business world and its corporate culture encroachment into higher education could produce negative repercussions from such a marriage. Is it possible that incivility might be a repercussion? Morgan State University counsel Julie Goodwin alluded to employer-employee disputes and the discrimination that often follows in any workplace. Might such disputes be uncivil? The debates over invention, technology transfer, and intellectual property rights as they relate to the university were raised by David Williams II, law professor and vice chancellor at Vanderbilt. He questioned the legitimate place of these new concerns within the university mission. Although we do not know everything about faculty incivility in the academic workplace, we do recognize that our academic world is changing faster than the academic culture and organizational governance structure can accommodate; thus, we can expect some reaction or repercussion, and we cannot expect it be all positive.

We use *faculty incivility* in the book in its broadest sense to address bullying, mobbing, camouflaged aggression, and harassment in the academic workplace. In order to understand the effect these behaviors have had and continue to have on faculty, we used a snowball sampling technique to identify men and women faculty members who have witnessed faculty incivility as observers or victims. Although we spent a great deal of time researching the topic in the library, we use our peers' anecdotal information to support and highlight what we found in the readings and in previous studies of general workplace harassment. We searched to find theories to support uncivil behavior, conceptual frameworks to illustrate the presence of these myriad behaviors, and analytical works to expound on the possible causes and effects of incivility among faculty. In addition, the two of us, who have worked in higher education for a combined sixty years, have witnessed and experienced incivility as faculty during our respective tenures. Our stories are similar to those of our peers. In fact, it was our own experiences with incivility and bullying that generated the idea for this book, but we soon realized that the instances are as unique as the people involved.

The chapters that follow are divided into three parts. Part One is foundational. We define incivility and what constitutes uncivil people in Chapter One. We demonstrate in Chapter Two how higher education through history has generated, supported, and rewarded uncivil acts. Although our premise in the book is structural and sociocultural, we devote Chapter Three to characteristics of proneness or predisposition to individual incivility, aggression, and bullying. Through our framework based on Denise Salin's model (2003) that illustrates why incivility exists in the workplace, we build a case for the organizational governance structure (Chapter Four) and academic work culture (Chapter Five) as fertile ground for uncivil behavior. Salin noted in her model that forces impinging on the workplace increase the likelihood of uncivil behavior.

Drawing on the historical changes in higher education that have brought conflict to the structure and culture of academe, we offer reasons in Part Two that incivility in all its forms might be on the rise. Chapter Six deals with the new groups that have entered academe, challenging the status quo and inadvertently disrupting the traditions of a long-standing homogeneous majority. Chapter Seven captures the more recent shift from traditional academic values to more corporate norms as the academic culture begins to look more like and exhibit the values of a corporate entity while attempting to still look like the culture of old.

In Chapters Eight and Nine in Part Three, we offer suggestions from other researchers, our research, and our colleagues for dealing with incivility, aggression, bullying, and mobbing in the academic workplace. In the Epilogue, we draw the elements together and offer food for thought. Along the way, faculty victims of incivility tell their stories to personalize the concepts and give meaning to the conceptual framework.

Darla J. Twale
Barbara M. De Luca

The Authors

Darla Twale is professor of education at the University of Dayton, where she coordinates the higher education administration strand of the doctorate in educational leadership program. She is currently on leave and is consulting with and directing a new online Ed.D. program in educational leadership for the Union Institute and University in Cincinnati. She holds degrees in sociology from Geneva College, Duquesne University, and the University of Pittsburgh. Her Ph.D. in higher education administration is also from the University of Pittsburgh. She spent eleven years at Auburn University teaching and coordinating the doctoral program in educational leadership before moving to Dayton.

Twale has over fifty articles in refereed journals, two book chapters, and seventy conference presentations. She is a coauthor of *Socialization of Graduate and Professional Students: A Perilous Passage* (Weidman, Twale, & Stein, 2001). While reviewing regularly or as an ad hoc reviewer for several journals, *Journal of College and University Student Housing*, *Journal of Research in Education*, *International Journal of Doctoral Studies*, *Journal of Higher Education*, and *Sex Roles*, she also serves as editor of the *Journal of Research in Education* and serves on the board of the Eastern Educational Research Association.

Barbara De Luca is an associate professor in educational leadership at the University of Dayton. She received her bachelor's degree from the University of Dayton, master's degree from Miami University (Ohio), and Ph.D. in economics and consumer economics from the Ohio State University. Her teaching and research are in the area of public K–12 finance. Her most recent publications focus on K–12 school finance issues facing the state of Ohio.

De Luca has extensive experience in a variety of positions and on numerous university committees. She founded the First Year Experience Program for first-year undergraduate students, at the University of Dayton and was its first director. She was the associate director of the University Honors and Scholars Program, a program for the top undergraduate students, and has served on the university's Awards Committee, the College of Arts and Sciences and School of Education, and Allied Professions academic programming committees. She was member or chairperson of the university's Faculty Hearing Committee for over ten years. She also served on the School of Education's Promotion and Tenure committee for several years.

Faculty Incivility

Part I

Laying the Foundation

The chapters in Part One explore faculty incivility using a conceptual framework to build a case as to how the organizational and governance structures and long-standing academic cultural norms may be the legitimizing factors in sustaining an academic bully culture. We approach the topic first from the perspective of knowing how to identify incivility, bullying, workplace harassment, mobbing, and camouflaged aggression. Civility and incivility are defined and placed in historical context in academe. We offer characteristics associated with aggressiveness and bully behavior. We then examine possible causes that may have spurred increased aggression as a result of institutional norms, governance and organizational structures, and academic culture. We offer an interactive, conceptual framework that depicts institutional (happening to individuals by other individuals), organizational (happening as the result of traditional university administrative design), and cultural (happening due to prevailing academic norms and values) factors that may invite or sustain these aggressive, uncivil behaviors.

1

Civility, Incivility, Bullying, and Mobbing in Academe

Warfare is common and no less deadly because it is polite.

J. Victor Baldridge

Have people been uncivil lately? Are they acting like playground bullies? The interpretation of what is civil and what is uncivil is in the perception of the receiver, not the sender (Barash, 2004). That is what makes the behavior so insidious, because the meaning behind the interaction could be anything from complete sincerity to sarcasm to flagrant manipulation. It could also be harassment, incivility, passive aggression, or bullying as translated by the receiver. The intent of the sender is insignificant.

Lynne Truss (2005) remarked recently about a prevailing feeling of selfishness, disrespect, self-absorption, and rudeness in America. She believed that if it is *my* place, then we follow *my* rules. She also posited that the increase in rudeness has precipitated an increase in books like Steve Carter's *Civility* (1998), Mark Caldwell's *A Short History of Rudeness* (1999), and Robert Putnam's *Bowling Alone* (2000). Long before those were published, however, Robert Sennett's *The Fall of Public Man* (1976) offered ways of explaining and fixing the problem of incivility. That it was a societal problem before he wrote about it and likely was a problem among faculty is indeed a reflection of society at large.

Sennett (1976) defined *civility* as "the activity which protects people from each other and yet allows them to enjoy each other's company" (p. 264). However, he also said that to be civil in polite society requires assuming a facade. This facade separates one from the typical power and conflict normally encountered and avoided in work situations. Goffman (1959) said "colleagues . . . share a community of fate," as they speak the same language and get to know each other's strengths and weaknesses (p. 160). The civil colleague maintains poise and self-control around colleagues or uses "impression management" to save the situation (p. 160). In other words, we use facades to maintain civility even as adverse feelings may be brewing beneath the surface.

Ferriss (2002) characterized civility with words like *decorum, manners, deportment,* and *politeness.* Furthermore, civility is also influenced by personal affect or reaction to the actions of another. The lack of these positive reactions and interactions indicates the presence of incivility. The presence of policy and legislation on sexual harassment is positive and has indeed decreased such acts, but not necessarily eliminated them. Uncivil acts still occur between academics, and perhaps more often than we care to admit.

Why do people bully? People's insecurity in themselves, lack of self-confidence, jealousy, inability to deal with life problems they may not wish to share, inability to deal with problems others know about but which they cannot deal with. — Cheryl

---

Ferriss (2002) argued further that civility or incivility is mitigated or filtered through culture, that is, customs, folkways, mores, and other sociocultural traditions and expectations. Each culture has these, and so does each workplace, where they differ from place to place and even department to department. Learning the subtle nuances of an academic culture is daunting because some of the information is purposefully hidden from view despite indications to the contrary. To keep cultural acts hidden is a subtle form of incivility; secrecy permits control, and control contributes to a culture of incivility.

Historically, civil behavior was maintained by social control mechanisms. Citizens came to realize that civility toward one another superseded disagreement. In order to maintain the culture, organization, society, and social order, decency and mannerly behavior prevailed despite frequent splintering and minor differences (Peck, 2002). Although conceptual and theoretical debates are necessary and healthy for personal and professional development, we suggest that a facade of social order and control often masks an underlying current of the general rudeness that prevails throughout society in general and the academy in particular.

Civility in Context

Civility/incivility has been interpreted as a semantic differential. This continuum configuration calculates the position of civil versus uncivil by factoring in the cultural setting, which dictates how well the civil response is accepted or tolerated with regard to one's occupational role or position in the hierarchy. We can determine just how civil or uncivil an action is by monitoring our tolerance level for each particular act as it relates to us. In terms of affect, Ferriss (2002) found those who are more civil practice greater self-control, self-restraint, and self-discipline.

In his study, Ferriss (2002) found age or lifetime to be a factor in civility, as incivility has increased slightly from the previous generation. Civility increases as one ages but does not necessarily increase as a result of education level or environment. Consider this: our parents were likely civil to the Fuller Brush man, the Hoover vacuum cleaner salesman, and the Avon lady. Some of us still remain civil to telemarketers when they call and interrupt our dinner. We are civil largely based on sociocultural custom. However, telemarketing, by the very nature of its anonymity and our personal devaluation of this occupation, seems to encourage people to be less civil to these workers than our parents were to them or were to door-to-door salespeople decades ago. Over time it is possible that by standards of previous generations, we are uncivil, but by Generation Xers and future generations, our current behaviors will probably be judged less harshly than we judge ourselves.

Members of various social groups judge behavior as proper or improper, civil or uncivil. One's current position or power base in an organization or group determines the vantage point from where one comes to judge what is civil or uncivil behavior. A determination that nothing is wrong, however, probably indicates that nothing will be done to correct any incivility (Montgomery, Kane, & Vance, 2004), allowing the uncivil act to gain acceptance. The act may be subtle or even hidden from view, but it is there nevertheless. As Ferriss (2002) pointed out, what is civil and proper in one place or time may not be as civil and proper in another place or time. Goffman (1963) called this "situational determinism." We cannot stress enough that regardless of time, place, or intent, the definition of the situation as civil or uncivil is left up to the victim of the action, not the perpetrator or actor (Thomas, 1923).

Sennett (1976) acknowledged two types of incivility: the incivility of charismatic leaders who act different once they are in power and the incivility of an insular, inclusive, fraternal, communal group faced with intrusion from new members unlike themselves. He added,

> Outsiders, unknowns, unlikes, become creatures to be shunned; the personality traits the community shares become ever more exclusive; the very act of sharing becomes even more centered upon decisions about who can belong and who cannot . . . . Fraternity has become empathy for a select group of people allied with rejection of those not within the local circle. This rejection

creates demands for autonomy that the outside world itself changes . . . . Fragmentation and internal division is the very logic of this fraternity, as the units of people who really belong get smaller and smaller. It is a version of fraternity which leads to fratricide [pp. 265–266].

Academe seems to be a breeding ground for uncivil behavior toward outsiders. This is the case only if those already in the "fraternity" get to vote on whether you meet with their approval. It has been my experience that it was and still is the men at the institution who refuse to accept my unorthodox, albeit no less legitimate, qualifications. I did not graduate with the "proper" degree, and my previous experience was not within the acceptable range to be included as a member of the "fraternity." Because of this, the "boys" refuse to acknowledge my education background and continually dismiss my contributions and abilities. They are, you understand, superior and in control, and I am different. Furthermore, they did not get to "vote" on me. In a unique situation, I was offered my current position without a vote of the department. — Kathy

---

Phillips and Smith (2003) define *incivility* as being "rude or inconsiderate," showing disrespectfulness, and not maintaining "deference and demeanor" in public (p. 85). They also distinguished between multiple types of incivility, such as the physical incivility of vandalism and the social incivility of fighting. These were further distinguished from a third type, *invisible incivility*, which violates norms of social behavior but is less easily detected or acknowledged.

Incivility is bound to happen. After all, we are strangers meeting other strangers. We might regard some actions as uncivil because they contrast sharply with our traditional cultural norms of behavior, even though the same behavior is regarded as acceptable in another cultural setting.

Defining Incivility in the Workplace

Salin (2003) noted that specific work environments and specific characteristics of workers attracted to a work environment have the potential to spawn and support aggressiveness. A hostile work environment is the result of power imbalances that lead to workplace aggression, camouflaged aggression, workplace incivility, or workplace bullying. Salin offered additional behaviors to illustrate the phenomenon—silent treatment, micromanaging, demotion, and being given less responsibility—and distinguished between physical violence and interpersonal issues. When these behaviors persist over a long period of time, a bully or mob culture is allowed to develop and flourish (Westhues, 2005).

Because their incivility was not checked early, the "brotherhood" has continued to bully, dictating who gets first choice of courses, class times, and class locations years later. — Kathy

---

Montgomery, Kane, and Vance (2004) asked, Who has to be incensed and/or how many people have to be incensed for a behavior to be considered uncivil? For persons like faculty who share the same social climate and live by the same social norms, one would presume that they as insiders would evaluate behaviors similarly. However, personal and social thresholds for incivility differ. It depends on who violated whom, when, where, how, how often, and why. More specifically, if the actors are from the same group, the violation is viewed differently than if they are not. If the violator is an administrator, for instance, and the victim is not, the violation may not be perceived as uncivil by the administrator. By the same token, administrative inaction wittingly or unwittingly sanctions future perpetuation of incivility not only between subordinates and superiors but perhaps among peers as well.

I was an outsider to education, not having come the traditional route. I was not initiated in the higher ed culture. I had to relearn what to do. Being in a school of education is like being in high school. They [faculty] form cliques just as they did in high school. They never left that environment. They did not have their beliefs and assumptions tested in another environment. People who are successful in schools are system dependent — it lets them know what, where, and how. They cannot deal with uncertainty . . . . Things were predictable each day; even disruptions were predictable. — Caroline

Over time, we may be desensitized to certain acts of incivility that would incense a newcomer. Some behaviors may exist but be invisible to those not looking for or expecting them. Thompson and Louque (2005) discussed accounts of demoralizing incidents, racial slurs, cultural insensitivity, and constant criticism from administrators in their published research study. In the "culture of arrogance," leaders often overlook or dismiss opportunities to resolve problems because socialization into that culture dictates otherwise. Problems were often ignored, covered up, or claimed to be nonexistent in the first place.

The organization is only as stable as the people at the top. So these people try to get you to believe *you*, not the organization, are the problem. But the organization *is* the problem. It becomes normalized, and you begin to believe you are abnormal. That is how people in this organization were acting, and I was not picking up on the cues as quickly as I should have. — Caroline

Montgomery, Kane, and Vance (2004) found females were more likely than males to identify particular behaviors as inappropriate.

They found that male and female faculty have differing thresholds for inappropriate or uncivil behaviors. In most cases, those who identify with the victim by race or by gender were more likely to side with the victim. The same sympathy principle applied to the perpetrator.

Civility and Incivility in Academe

Campbell (2000) charged that faculty have "flawed moral compasses, from ethical codes gone awry" (p. 154). Unless we realize that, it will destroy academe, he predicted. In fact, faculty have "tenaciously held and zealously protected" the status quo (p. 161). We explore that contention further.

Incivility in the Department

Hume (2003) pointed out that department faculty have become so civil that they often fail to recognize that some tenured colleagues no longer contribute their fair share to teaching, research, or service obligations. Perhaps other ill feelings toward colleagues are subverted, that is, channeled through other avenues. In the meantime, department colleagues pretend all is well through their civility and adopted facade, for to call the deadwood issue into question might be thought of as mean-spirited by colleagues. It would, however, be well intentioned, given that noncontributing faculty use up limited resources and perhaps do students a disservice.

Hume (2003) further characterized faculty as possessing political self-interests. To push those self-interests would mean that other individual faculty interests would be invaded. This would not support the thin veil of civility. Such well-meaning idealistic suggestions would be summarily dismissed, and the colleague making the disparaging suggestion would perhaps be ostracized as "different," "difficult," or "not collegial" by senior colleagues.

During a departmental meeting to award level 2 graduate faculty status to a candidate, another faculty member and I voted no, while the majority voted yes. We argued that the candidate did not meet the requirements, but the spokesperson for the majority reminded us that the candidate had a family and had just assumed a mortgage; therefore, if we did not support him, he would have to leave the university, and he had a family to support. I argued that he was not doing his job, and I think there were more people in the department who agreed with us dissenters but were afraid to buck the spokesperson. As a female viewed as trying to "destroy" the career of a male colleague, and a home owner at that, I was labeled bitchy and vindictive and as holding a grudge against this man. — Abby

Incivility and the Classroom

Braxton and Bayer (1999) noted that incivility in the classroom has risen, but they do not attribute total blame to student brashness or general increases in campus or societal violence. They contended that the classroom behavior of faculty toward students may be problematic and precipitous. For example, they regarded chronic tardiness and absenteeism, off-color humor, demeaning comments, public humiliation, and gross profanity in the classroom as incivility. Their premise was that if students were uncivil to faculty, perhaps it was linked to unprofessional faculty behavior because there is little regulation for classroom teaching.

I was teaching in a doctoral cohort my first year. One woman in the cohort screamed at me about how bad my syllabus was and how much work the course would be and that I should talk to my colleagues and they could tell me how to put a course together. . . . I was the interloper who entered after the cohort had been together for five semesters. Only one woman in the whole class supported me. They wrote e-mails to my chair and my mentor and my colleagues. The students are the customers, and maybe they are right. I was never able to control the class. I give students extensive feedback on papers, and I am the queen of turnaround time. The students in this class asked why I bothered . . . . Did I really believe they were going to read *my* comments? My scores in the class evaluation were low, and they said I should be fired. . . . My colleagues supported the student, whom they said was very bright and a good student. — Caroline

Faculty in the Braxton and Bayer (1999) study experienced difficulty agreeing on classroom behavior, that is, what one faculty member saw as unacceptable another dismissed as absent-minded or eccentric. Faculty responses to behaviors differed by gender, status, and tenure, which made it difficult to reach consensus on unacceptable classroom behaviors. Seasoned faculty with rank, status, and prominence tended to impose higher standards for faculty and felt comfortable enforcing them, perhaps through the peer review process. They concluded that if teaching is regarded as less important than research, incidents of classroom incivility would be expected and infractions stood a chance of being overlooked or dismissed. In other words, the culture and the structure of higher education would continue to tolerate and absorb such inappropriate behavior.

In both undergraduate and graduate school, I saw a number of incidents in which students were hostile to the professor. I just never understood it. How could they [the professors] tolerate it? I won't and don't tolerate hostile and uncivil behavior [from students]. However, if nothing is done about student incivility, then that lack of accountability emboldens others to go ahead with their bad behavior. — George

I recall one graduate class, this guy all semester made snide comments, and finally I had had it. I asked him to stay after class. I sat him down and asked, "Please let me know what you are thinking because I don't understand all the snide remarks, and I think it could be better if you talked to me about it." He said, "We *all* hate you, I haven't learned a thing, blah, blah, blah." So I just said, "Thank you for your feedback, as I was curious as to what you were thinking." Instead of coming to me for help, he came at me with anger. — Allison

---

Incivility as Manipulation

Braithwaite (2001) defined aggressive behavior as largely "an outward expression of an internal emotion or an action created by circumstances" (p. 22). He reported that a few people find aggression (even passive aggression) helpful as a means to manipulate others to achieve desired ends. Primary causes of aggression include an innate human quality stemming from frustration, a learned behavioral response to positive or reinforcing stimuli, and an environmental response or societal stereotype that dictates unequal social status. In fact, workplace aggression includes behaviors such as exploitation, coercive power in management, machismo, power plays, and defamation of character (Hannabus, 1998).

I was responsible for giving a faculty colleague a piece of information. I also had an associate dean ask for another piece of information, so I attended to the dean's request before that of my colleague. The colleague came into my office and went on a tirade about how I dragged everybody down. She said I did not do my responsibilities. Every button I had was pushed by her tirade, and she was probably justified because I didn't get her work done in the manner in which she wanted it done. I felt I needed to do the associate dean's request first. This incident affected me so deeply that I did not feel comfortable working with her ever again. I respected her work, but the fact that she treated me this way was too much for me to handle. — Lucille

---

Workplace aggressors compete, gossip, divulge confidences, offer criticism publicly, patronize, find fault, and overload colleagues with work. Hannabus (1998) tried to make the distinction between bully and bossy and reached the conclusion that if either gets results for the organization through the use of these aggressive behaviors, it will be regarded as effective and remain in vogue. Some bullies project charming personas in public situations to cover their covert vindictiveness.

A colleague has passed me in the halls or on the stairways many times and never speaks to me; he puts his head down or does an about-face and heads in the other direction. However, when I see him pass other colleagues, especially the men, he speaks to them. On one occasion when he was walking with a campus administrator, he spoke to me. I hate being patronized by this guy, then being ignored, and, what is worse, I don't think he thinks he is doing anything wrong. — Abby

---

Incivility as Retaliation and Indifference

Lawyer Ann Franke (2005) insisted that workplace retaliation would "surpass discrimination as the most severe employment problem in higher education" (p. B14). She considered retaliatory harassment as incivility. Common reactions include seeking support from others by stressing just one side of the whole story, ignoring or dismissing the complaint, and marginalizing the complainer. Retaliation can take several forms that are camouflaged in the workplace, such that it is difficult for the accuser or accused to justify or refute.

The ex-superintendent found out I didn't support him when he was hired. He was angry because of the questions I asked him in the interview that he was unable to answer. When I returned after my leave, I had no graduate courses to teach, although I had had them before I left. I was blacklisted from teaching grad courses. I have undergrads. I am no longer listed in the grad catalogue. I am a full professor and tenured and at the institution over a decade. — Ben

---

Namie and Namie (2003) alluded to the fact that in some work environments, bystanders know what is going on, but they usually do nothing to help victims for fear of retaliation. A culture of incivility begins to support the bully through reinforcement and eventually becomes engrained in the existing academic culture. Targeted victims usually internalize the problem, isolate themselves, and choose not to share privately or air publicly instances of bullying, mobbing, incivility, or harassment. Whether the silence is totally out of fear or out of embarrassment, frustration, or importance is difficult to determine. Silence is also associated with feelings of powerlessness and lack of knowledge on navigating the university grievance process, if there is one.

My institution tends to reward and promote those colleagues who demonstrate incivility . . . . I see coalitions developing across campus, within departments, and among those who have designs for power/control. I think that making others uncomfortable and feeling unwelcome is a method of silencing voices. Who wants to put up with that crap in a toxic workplace? It is far easier to just go to one's office, shut the door, and get the work done. It's lonely and frustrating, but it is the path of least resistance. — George

I just decided to do my own thing. After trying to navigate through the institutional grievance process and learning it was really designed for staff rather than faculty, I chose to just quietly do my job, avoiding collegiality and active participation in department and division activities, be they academic, social, or otherwise. I just became other focused, *other* meaning "other than the internal culture." I focused on my class and my research, and that's it. — Kathy

---

Incivility as Bullying

These behaviors are indicative of bullying (Appleton, Briggs, Rhatigan, & Anderson, 1978):

- Indulging in self-promotion

- Showing intolerance or disrespect to others

- Giving lame alibis or rationalizations for actions

- Procrastinating to avoid fixing relationships or chasms

- Demonstrating temper and hostility during individual or group confrontations

- Demonstrating poor knowledge of human and interpersonal relations

- Indulging in professional misconduct such as breaking confidentiality, harboring rumors, and playing favorites

- Avoiding taking a stand when one is needed to correct a wrong

- Employing ineffective strategies to correct problems and inadvertently causing more problems

Bullying challenges the limits of civility. To be civil means to be able to balance and contain personal desires, especially when these desires are in conflict with one another. In times of conflict, stress, or extreme pressure, however, the bully aligns personal interests to his or her own agenda in the belief that he or she is acting for the greater good of others or the organization. The individual acting as a bully lacks self-control and directs his or her irrational emotions toward others, who receive and interpret the behavior as an uncivil act (Peck, 2002).

We think of bullying as child's play (Henry, 2004; Namie & Namie, 2003; Olafsson & Johannsdottir, 2004) and not something that adults do. But child bullies do not always outgrow their bullying behavior.

Abdennur (2000) and Coyne, Craig, and Smith-Lee Chong (2004) see bullying as inherently societal and organizational, such that adult bullies are encouraged by the institution to continue this behavior. Specifically, the same tension that manifests itself as uncivil behavior on the playground exists in the greater society. In fact, these researchers believe it is gaining increased presence in the workplace. In addition, the same dynamic that permitted the bully to reign on the playground is probably present in the organization and the culture to sustain it there, but in a more grown-up manifestation, perhaps under the guise of civil facades. Klein (2005) stated that as on the schoolyard, bullies are impotent without supporters or a support system.

Prolonged workplace incivility and bullying can sustain a bully culture. In addition, in academe, the governance structure and the hierarchical organization may serve as an incubator for the establishment or maintenance of a bully culture.

If no one listened to that deceitful committee chair or if some-one investigated deeply enough to uncover what really happened in those committee deliberations, there would have been no one supporting the unscrupulous behavior and, consequently, no reason to continue the behavior. The consequent incivility by those who "trusted" the bully and themselves became bullies would never have festered. — Kathy

---

Perhaps tensions rise over the regard for status as a sought-after commodity. Tension may simply grow out of upheaval and change (Ferris, 2004; Hoel, Faragher, & Cooper, 2004; Hoel & Salin, 2003; Olafsson & Johannsdottir, 2004). Changes at work can add to that pressure, especially if workers feel they, their values, and their position are being threatened (Davenport, Schwartz, & Elliott, 1999). With the introduction of corporate culture into academe, decreased support for public higher education from the states, and budget tightening on all campuses, tensions can mount (Washburn, 2005; Zemsky, Wegner, & Massy, 2005). We couple this with the fact that faculty and their sandbox politics compete for status, rank, merit pay, travel money, and space in journals.

Deliberate or unconscious, verbal or nonverbal, isolated or repetitive, uncivil acts of bullying like these are unwanted by their victims (Jennifer, Cowie, & Ananiadou, 2003; Ferris, 2004; Lewis, 2004; Abdennur, 2000; Hadikin & O'Driscoll, 2000; Henry, 2004; Heim & Murphy, 2001; Hoel, Faragher, & Cooper, 2004; Keashly & Jagatic, 2003; McCarthy & Mayhew, 2004; Olafsson & Johanns-dottir, 2004; Peyton, 2003; Rayner, Hoel, & Cooper, 2002; Smith, Singer, Hoel, & Cooper, 2003):

- Manipulating and intimidating the seemingly powerless

- Divulging confidential information

- Insulating and protecting negative behaviors while ignoring positive contributions

- Assigning overloads coupled with unrealistic expectations

- Using public humiliation, insults, innuendo, rumor, slander, libel, sarcasm, backstabbing, talking down to, and lies

- Excluding, alienating, marginalizing, ostracizing, silencing, patronizing, and scapegoating others

- Unfairly treating, hounding, micromanaging, undermining, and unfairly criticizing

- Distributing resources unequally by supervisors

- Withholding resources and information from colleagues and subordinates or failing to render a decision

- Belittling or dismissing others' valid opinions and ideas

- Deceiving, using passive-aggressive behaviors, and flaunting power and authority

- Eroding another's self-confidence and self-esteem

- Not correcting false information

- Involving others as allies who become complicit in these behaviors

- Shunning, denying someone's existence, questioning one's judgment or decisions, and continually and consistently interrupting

We recognize that incivility and bullying may not be solely an act of an individual. Given the committee governance structure in higher education, the strength of the academic culture, and the notion that bullies need support from others to be successful, a bully often acts in consort with others, that is, a mob.

Incivility as Mobbing Behavior

Serial bullies, or habitual bullies, can always find justification for their behavior. When it becomes such an indistinguishable part of the organization, Hannabus (1998) calls it "corporate bullying." Westhues (2005) refers to the phenomenon as "mobbing": a prolonged, repeated series of acts on coworkers or supervisors. Mobbing encompasses various forms of bully behavior. It appears to be polite, civil aggression or criticism, but its forced invisibility renders it more toxic. Mobbing includes the starting of unfounded rumors and slander and demotion or loss of assignment without just cause; the victims are thereby ostracized, shunned, or marginalized by a group of bullies. Davenport, Schwartz, and Elliott (1999) noted that the ultimate goals of mobbing are to "dominate, subjugate, and eliminate" (p. 23). Mobbing is a special category of workplace harassment that these researchers believe may affect as much as 15 percent of the working population. Hoel and Salin (2003) estimate that bullying (or mobbing) may affect as much as 20 percent of the workforce.

In the workplace, mobbing takes on a five-step process (the last step would be difficult to impose in academe): (1) conflict with victim, (2) aggressive acts toward victim, (3) involvement of management, (4) victim labeled as difficult, and (5) firing of victim (Davenport, Schwartz, & Elliott, 1999). Davenport, Schwartz, and Elliott have credited mobbing behaviors with attacking employee "dignity, integrity, and credibility" (p. 41). The victim endures humiliation, feeling set up, at fault, and subsequently misinterpreted. Mobbing can persist only because bullies have allies and networks; these allies constitute the "mob." Plots are engineered to eliminate or disarm troublesome employees who perhaps stand in the way of others' agendas. Davenport, Schwartz, and Elliott posited that although the unique culture and structure of the academic organization may support mobbing inadvertently, it is no less deadly an extent for some faculty victims (see also Westhues, 2005). In academe, because tenured faculty are difficult to dismiss, an uncivil mob may resort to isolation, slander, invisibility, shunning, and elimination from governance activities as a way to encourage the victim to leave on his or her own. Readings (1996) acknowledged that "few communities are more petty and vicious than university faculties" (p. 180).

My chair became angry over a trivial issue and made a federal case that lasted for years. — Ben

I have experience not doing what I've been told, because it goes against best practice. The dean gets over it, but has also looked to more malleable, less expert colleagues in different arenas to do the job he wants done. I always figured they hired me for my expertise, not using it as someone else understands it to be. — Sue

---

Identifying the Uncivil, the Bully

Namie and Namie (2003) typify work environments where bullying emerges and remains because administrators do not see the problems or simply deny problems exist; institutions focus on image rather than inner substance; secretive behaviors surround hiring and firing; administrators bypass faculty channels to push their agendas; and poor communication or miscommunication means that symbolic messages are sent and received differently by different people or groups of people.

Individuals have psychological needs that are met through bullying others. These individuals may be controlling, power hungry, neurotic, insecure, pompous, egotistical, socially dysfunctional, narcissistic, jealous, or self-aggrandizing. Despite their bully characteristics, they find that seeking allies is easier than working alone (Davenport, Schwartz, & Elliott, 1999). Strategically, the best place to search for allies is among leaders. The second-best option is to seek a leadership role or position.

Through careful manipulation, bullies may inadvertently be mistaken for leaders (French & Raven, 1960). Normal, average-behaving colleagues who have an opportunity to exert pressure on another colleague for some reward may be enticed to exhibit uncivil behavior toward that colleague. Therefore, given the power of the dangling carrot, a bully could be created. Leadership roles or positions place the bully in a unique position, referred to as the catbird seat, where rewards may be forthcoming.

According to Campbell (2000), authority figures often "see through naughty schemes but look the other way" (p. 31). It may be easier to do that than deal with real problems. This avoidance may also stem from the fact that administrators and faculty have other things they see as more pressing. Although such behavior is understandable, ignoring it is not acceptable. Perhaps leaders have no idea what to do about such problems when they encounter them because no repertoire of proven solutions exists. Campbell would refer to this conspiracy of silence as the essence of the dry rot in academe; it avoids the hard truths that surround reality.

Chronic bully personalities pose challenges to leaders trying to deal with them (Namie & Namie, 2003). Bullies may seek allies among leaders. Strong administrations may appear to be uncivil, dictatorial bullies to their faculties. Weak or laissez-faire leadership, though not uncivil, can inadvertently instigate incivility through inaction. These leaders may also be unable to stop bully behaviors and mobs once they begin (Davenport, Schwartz, & Elliott, 1999).

There was this married couple in the department who had a strong power base. That is probably why we had several department chairs while I was there. When we finally hired a nice fellow from outside the university to chair the department, this couple piled on the charm with him right after he moved into his office. He shared that fact with me and a colleague, who both told him that it was not charm and hospitality; rather, they expected loyalty from him in return and would be back for it in due time. He was skeptical of what we said, but probably a year or so later, he acknowledged that we were right. I gave him a lot of credit for saying that to us. They perceived him as an easy target and sought to take advantage of his good nature. He caught on eventually. — Abby

The department hired an ex-superintendent who has no people skills and has been released from his last three jobs. While I was on leave, this person was promoted to graduate program director and also hired his buddy. The sidekick was much more suave, though. They displaced a well-respected graduate program with one that has little to do with best practices. He hired adjuncts to teach classes, but if they cross him, they get no courses. He micromanages, downplays, and tries to throw every faculty meeting off course. He lies, and the chair knuckles under to them. — Ben

Victims of Incivility, Bullying, and Mobbing

Using a committee structure to inadvertently entwine others in the mob process without their realizing it signifies the presence of mob behavior. Mobbing through committee decisions camouflages and insulates the real bully or singular instigator (Davenport, Schwartz, & Elliott, 1999). Klein (2005) regarded mobbing or bullying as following multiple episode patterns. In other words, isolated events may not be detected by the victim, but several events related to one another are a clearer pattern.

I remember very clearly a situation of bullying resulting from a colleague divulging confidences. The result of a committee chair divulging confidential committee deliberations was devastating. And as though violating confidences wasn't bad enough, I have excellent reason to believe he was untruthful about what he "divulged" regarding both the nature of the discussions and his role in the proceedings. What leads me to believe this? Well, when the results of the deliberations proved to be unsatisfactory, the makeup of the committee changed, and the continued incivility shown the deposed committee members was outrageous. — Kathy

---

Complicating matters are colleagues who in social situations appear collegial, congenial, and supportive to the victim but in private become just the opposite. The victims are excluded, disenfranchised, silenced, overlooked, or ignored.

Faculty perpetrators who perceive themselves as less mobile in their career often subvert their displeasure through perhaps improper means (Gouldner, 1957, 1958). Faculty victims who are less mobile and more reliant on the institution for salary and benefits seldom speak up about their plight. Despite being overworked and underappreciated, faculty victims typically fail to use the channels prescribed by policy (Austin & Gamson, 1983; Twale & Lane, 2006), highlighting their powerlessness and fear.

Targets likely to be mobbed or bullied are people who are different or threaten the status quo. Colleagues who unwittingly buck the system or challenge long-established patterns or values may be likely targets for bullies and mobs. At first, victims of bullying and mobbing probably trust their colleagues and may not be aware they are being targeted. Those new to higher education are perhaps too naive to realize that seemingly well-meaning colleagues would be uncivil toward them or that the academic culture and organizational structure may have built-in mechanisms to permit bullying or mobbing (Davenport, Schwartz, & Elliott, 1999).

I recall this schoolwide faculty meeting chaired by the dean, and being a new faculty member, I was appalled: untenured male professors berated full-tenured female professors, and this was just a couple of years ago. My department meetings were horrible. People screamed at one another for hours. Setting dates/times to meet candidates in a search process would incite battles. . . . I cried in my office after faculty meetings. — Caroline

---

To be isolated means to be labeled a pariah, an academic untouchable. People are instructed and encouraged to avoid the target's company lest they be labeled similarly. When these more covert procedures fail to encourage the victim to leave the institution, overt attacks may occur. From these overt and covert actions comes invalidation: the victim is discredited, thus raising suspicions regarding many of the victim's previous actions.

[I feel] marginalized by the dean; made to feel through verbal comments "when are you leaving." Being told "what you will do" on return to the faculty from sabbatical leave — especially given a "job description" without any consultation. In another incident, I was accused [by the female dean] of making a crude ethnic remark toward an Asian individual (I did not) and was sent an official letter indicating that any further disparagement of ethnic groups on my part would result in severe discipline. — Doug

---

Colleagues seem to criticize many things the victim does or says. As a result, Klein (2005) attributed this sequence of behaviors as eventually leading to differential treatment of the victim, which ultimately affects merit, tenure, and promotion decisions. He noted that different standards are applied to the disenfranchised that range from poor evaluations and smaller salary increments to tenure denial.

I am learning more about my colleague. She comes on strong sometimes . . . strong minded and opinionated, and she may be perceived by others as the bully and they are just responding to *her* behavior. She is not in control here as an untenured faculty. People are not in agreement with her, so they see her doing things that are inappropriate. She is interpreting her experience that she has with them from her previous environment. — Allison

---

Feeling victimized can be a cause for further victimization, that is, victims may display more vulnerability. Milgram (1963) noted from his studies that to ensure greater social distance, other rational acts accompanied initial victimization. Aggressors play a blame game such that the victim is the perpetrator, deserving of the continued aggression. It is easier to act in heinous ways against the victim once the victim has been isolated and dehumanized. In time, bullies and mobs experience desensitization to their acts and their victims, such that once the original sting is gone, bullies experience forgetfulness. Out-of-sight is out-of-mind.

My female chair tells the faculty one thing and this one male faculty member another. When this man did what she allowed the female faculty to do, he was called on the carpet. He is not tenured and chose not to fight it even though he had a case. We (the rest of the faculty) don't understand why she treats us one way and him another. This guy doesn't pose a threat to her. I urged him to bring it to grievance. He would not follow through because he wants tenure and would rather be bitched at. On another occasion she took him to the provost, and he didn't fight that either. He came to me to ask how he should fill out a specific form in hopes that he doesn't get into trouble with her again. He has been crapped on since he started, but he keeps marching along. She doesn't treat the females that way. — Allison

---

Victims have usually done something unknowingly to arouse the bully or the mob. These acts range from simply being hired to challenging philosophically something someone said. No matter how scholarly or civil the challenge, going against the normal flow or rhythm of the department, school, or university culture can have deleterious effects for the challenger. Despite the fact that the intellectual challenge is valid, the bully takes personal affront to the act. If the academic culture or organizational structure is conducive, the bully or the mob finds justification for their behavior and likely repeats it. Victims become revictimized by the bully or the mob and also by subsequent bouts of their own self-doubt (Davenport, Schwartz, & Elliott, 1999).

We want to make clear that "bullying is not about what the perpetrator meant; it is about what the recipient felt" (Peyton, 2003, p. 84). Therefore, likely victims of bullying are those perceived to be shy, vulnerable, powerless, defenseless, marginal people and those having low self-esteem (Hoel, Faragher, & Cooper, 2004; Jennifer, Cowie, & Ananiadou, 2003). Researchers view the phenomenon as more of a power than a gender issue (Hoel, Einarsen, & Cooper, 2003; Rayner, Hoel, & Cooper, 2002). However, Smith, Singer, Hoel, and Cooper (2003) found that women are more likely than men to be bully victims in the workplace (Hoel, Faragher, & Cooper, 2004; Olafsson & Johannsdottir, 2004). Given the disparity in gender of more senior male faculty and more junior and part-time female faculty, odds are that more cases of incivility are reported by women than men. When the gender distributions are more balanced, the proportion of victims and bullies of either gender is also likely to be more balanced.

Because of the covert nature of some of the uncivil actions of bullying and mobbing and the fear of reprisal by victims, victims often suppress the resulting emotions and do not fully reveal to others what has happened (Lewis, 2004; White, 2004). Suppression is as likely to be by both men and women but perhaps for different reasons. Men are more likely to be embarrassed and women more fearful. Sustained over time, these emotions manifest themselves in physiological and psychological difficulties for the individual victims and their organizations. Incivility and bullying also affect empowerment, competency, and motivation; they are disempowering (Hoel, Faragher, & Cooper, 2004; Lewis, 2004; White, 2004).

After I had tenure and was a year or so away from going up for full [professor], I had the unfortunate ordeal of having to confront a doctoral student with her plagiarized term paper, documentation and all, and that I was taking her before the academic honesty committee. She ran to her dissertation "co-chairs." They each came to me individually. The first one asked me to reconsider, and the other one point-blank said, "If you take her to that committee, it will hurt *you* more than it will hurt her." I was stunned, but I also deserved full professor, and I knew what he meant: they would block it. So I worked out a deal where she would rewrite the paper. I hated to make that compromise. It was over a decade ago, and I still hate what I felt I had to do, and that was, compromise my integrity. Later they blocked my promotion anyway. That hurt even more. — Abby

---

Conceptual Framework

Little scholarship exists on American workplace incivility, although studies have been conducted on aggressive behavior and bullying in European workplaces, mostly outside academe. Based on the reading of numerous studies on workplace aggression, we have blended an analysis of organization, governance, and culture. Denise Salin (2003) has developed a framework that is reflective of workplaces in general; it entwines several key areas that make incivility, bullying, and mobbing more likely to manifest themselves in a work environment. We have adapted her framework to be reflective of academe and the pressures facing faculty that make incivility, bullying, and mobbing possible. The structure of Parts One and Two of this book follows her framework, which is presented in Figure 1.1.

Salin (2003) uses "motivating structures and processes" to refer to the means offered in the form of incentives and positive reinforcements that encourage incivility, bullying, and mobbing behavior. In academe, those include the committee governance structure and the fact that faculty own the means of production that interfaces with the power imbalance, often fueling faculty-administrative tension. "Precipitating circumstances" are the "triggering circumstances" (p. 1217) that encourage incivility, bullying, and mobbing. We focus here on two general areas: corporate culture and the changing face of academe. "Enabling structures and processes" encompass what allows incivility, bullying, and mobbing to occur. In academe, we identify the strong academic culture that inadvertently supports isolation and ambiguity and the inherent stresses and tensions built into the faculty role. Salin posited that the presence of all these elements determines whether there is the opportunity for incivility and workplace aggression to exist. We agree that when these elements are present *and* existing bully behaviors are permitted or are rewarded in the culture and the structure, an academic bully culture will be permitted residence.

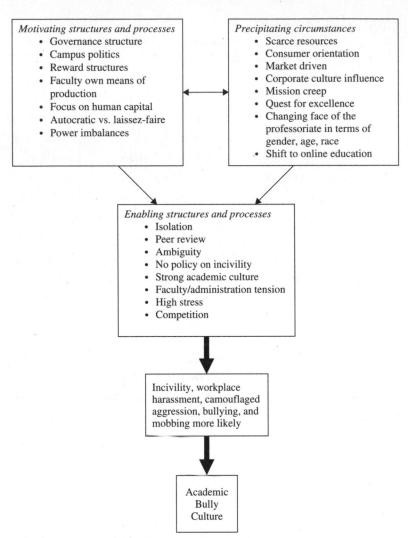

Figure 1.1. Conceptual Framework of Bullying

We hear some of these stresses and pressures in accounts from faculty colleagues. Because the nature of incivility is defined by the victim, these faculty members described incidents of incivility, bullying, and mobbing. We asked them about the structures and processes that were in place when these incidents occurred and how these contributed to the problem. In addition, we wanted to know how they felt, and if the bullying or mobbing was dealt with and resolved. We make no attempt to code or discuss prevailing themes expressed by these faculty members. Given the exploratory nature of this study, we are offering their anecdotes where they support the prevailing literature. These persons have experienced incivility, bullying, or mobbing behavior while employed in academe. Our hope is that what was once camouflaged will be brought into the light.

2

Incivility and the History
of Higher Education

*All history is only one long story to this effect: Men
have struggled for power over their fellow men in
order that they might win the joys of earth at the
expense of others, and might shift the burdens of life
from their own shoulders upon those of others.*
                                    William Graham Sumner

Incivility has roots in academe. This chapter takes the reader
through a brief history of higher education, one that has been
threaded overtly and covertly with instances of deception, incivility, bullying, bias, harassment, discrimination, inequity, and
inequality. The historical pattern indicates that some of these
unfortunate, and often ironic, instances likely were suppressed,
sanitized, ignored, overlooked, or simply mistaken for normal
behavior. These responses were done at the expense of others. This
chapter is organized around a series of academic struggles that have
affected higher education. To capture the beginning of incivility
we go back over 370 years to Harvard.

Ironically, one of Harvard's goals was to advance civility among
its gentlemen graduates. In fact, the goal of early colonial collegiate
education was to produce civil gentlemen, Christian men, and civic
magistrates. However, survival often required college overseers to
solicit money from benefactors under false pretenses. Both Harvard
College and the Virginia Company from England and Scotland

sought funds for education, especially for converting the Native Americans to Christianity. However, few Native American students were ever recruited, educated, or graduated from Harvard, the College of William and Mary, or Dartmouth. In fact to secure these royal charters, these institutions simply had to match the need for Indian education with the royals' willingness to fund such ventures. Nevertheless, each school's intention was always to produce white scholars rather than improve the life of American Indians. Native Americans were exploited by colonists in several fraudulent schemes to extort money under the guise of Christian philanthropy (Brubaker & Rudy, 1997; Cremin, 1970; Wright, 1997). So what was foundationally developed to produce civil gentleman was never wholly attempted or perhaps realized in the academic culture from the beginning, and it came at the expense of a group unable to realize how and how much they were continuing to be exploited.

Elitism Versus Merit Versus Democratization

Perhaps the best example of early academic philosophical disputes came as the educated white elite realized that education was being expanded to include intelligent males who were not necessarily rich. That quest for domination by the white elite was first challenged by clerics. Despite clergy domination of universities, the institution was still a college, not a church or a seminary. As a result, political and philosophical disputes arose as to the institution's place in addressing greater social issues (Herbst, 1976).

In the colonial period, the growth of the student subculture placed itself at odds with the faculty. Education was seen as a means of social control because it was designated to preserve the social class level and elite status of colonial gentlemen. Institutions were patriarchal and paternalistic, and colonial institutions practiced provincial isolation as a way to preserve knowledge and pass it along to select groups. Often the result was the production of an elite community of the learned.

With the advent of the Industrial Revolution, there were new images for higher education. Elitist models gave way to token inclusion of previously underrepresented groups. However, this mid- to late-nineteenth-century expansion did not mean the beginning of greater equality for those groups. The need for the United States to increase human capital did not ensure a concomitant increase or return on social and cultural capital, which was still in the hands of elite white males and factions of a recently emerging middle class (Perkin, 1997).

No longer purely elitist enterprises, more colleges saw enrollees come from more humble circumstances and some women. However, those with more modest means matriculated at local and regional institutions, not yet posing much threat to the Ivy League elitism (Potts, 1997). While first admitting women to higher education indicated "progress," offering that education in separate but unequal institutions legitimized subordination rather than promoted equality and accessibility for these new entrants (Palmieri, 1997). The typical women's college curriculum was largely a finishing school designed to occupy women's time while their male age-mates were obtaining a more substantive education. The Seven Sisters colleges prepared women to assume a proper wifely role to their professional husbands (Church & Sedlak, 1977).

A new culture of educated women nevertheless emerged in 1820 that affected attitudes toward women and challenged elitist male values. Too much education, it was believed, could affect feminine emotionalism, yet education was prescribed to capture women's natural role as caretaker and caregiver. In addition, common schools forced the need for teachers, and the Civil War forced the need for nurses. Equality, autonomy, and ambition were palatable (Palmieri, 1997) as long as they did not interfere with elitist male schooling.

Educated women constituted a "cultural motherhood" class. Separation of men and women in the classroom further portrayed the genders as unequal. Because the spirit of the Morrill Act of

1862 promoted the education of children of working-class parents, women sought preparation for social activism rather than for "cultural motherhood" (Gordon, 1997).

By the turn of the twentieth century, women entering college raised male suspicions even further with regard to their inclination to marry and raise a family rather than pursue a career. Backlashes against feminists began. The elite women attending college competed for spaces but were often supplanted by the emerging male immigrant population. The presence of immigrant males appeared far less intrusive to elite white males than the female presence. In fact, women were performing better than men in their classes, posing a threat to the long-standing male dominance in academe (Palmieri, 1997). Even with the addition of land grant universities after 1862, which offered a broader curriculum, women gravitated to the softer sciences and humanities curriculums. As a result, these courses became stigmatized as inferior to the harder and applied scientific fields that men were choosing.

Coeducation began as segregated education. Atypically, in the Wisconsin normal schools, both sexes shared a social, intellectual, and cocurricular life. The field of education for men and women of all races remained accessible, balanced, and inclusive. As normal schools began their evolution to state teachers' colleges and eventually, decades later, to regional comprehensive state universities, they mirrored the pattern at land grant universities. Men and women intellectually and socially parted ways as they assumed a more superior versus subordinate stance typical of the more paternalistic culture found in larger comprehensive public institutions (Ogren, 1997).

Prior to and especially following the Civil War, education for emancipated slaves included similar training for males and females as a means to improve social and economic conditions. However, postsecondary education opened more doors for black men than it did for black women. For black men to succeed in a white society, they inadvertently bought into the intellectual male dominance and female subordination philosophy that prevailed in higher education and white society at large (Perkins, 1997). As the gains that black and white females made in education were lost, a pattern was inadvertently being established and followed.

With the increased numbers of females in academe came an increase in sex bias, discrimination, and harassment in areas of hiring, tenure, promotion, salary, and benefits. Given a female and minority presence in academe and a glow of sunshine on these gender-related problems in academe, higher education commissions, task forces, research studies, journal articles, forums, and books were dedicated to policy change. Unfortunately, progress was slow, and frequent legal challenges slowed the movement even further (Robbins & Kahn, 1985).

Faculty Versus Changing Ideology

Professionalization among eighteenth- and nineteenth-century faculty was characterized by a dynamically transformed intellectual role superimposed on an increasingly complex institutional structure still under faculty construction (Finkelstein, 1997). Tension mounted as faculty assumed the dual roles of disciplinary professional and knowledge expert, as well as employee and production owner within a newly developing bureaucratic hierarchy. In addition, competition for decreasing opportunities in decision making in an attempt to maintain some modicum of power and control exacerbated tensions (Gruber, 1997). Faculty traditions were challenged. They learned that their work was subject to scrutiny and validation by their peers. Performance expectations for faculty seemed more uncertain or esoteric, causing faculty greater stress, tension, and consternation. Changes in institutional mission challenged faculty autonomy and the collegiality they once took for granted (Huber, 2002).

Rifts between faculty and students were also common. The situation emerging was referred to as "the awful chasm" (Veysey,

1965, p. 294). Faculty challenged the intellectual gap between the classless plow boys studying agriculture and the elite, cultured white gentlemen philosophizing in the traditional liberal arts. Students took the opportunity to denigrate and mock faculty for their stereotypical Mr. Chips–like persona in retaliation. Wechsler (1997) reminded us that all new groups that have entered white male–dominated, Christian-based higher education have always been met with suspicion and trepidation. For example, the attendance of work-oriented poor students on financial scholarship challenged wealthier white students whose goal was simply elite socialization. These two distinct groups managed their differences in order to address what they viewed as the potential horrors of coeducation. American education founded on Christian principles was challenged later by an influx of Jewish students. Perhaps this was less of a problem, but the fact remained that women constituted a significant portion of this group. In fact, college administrators welcomed Jews as academically astute students, but Christian students posed barriers to their social acceptance and inclusion.

While social status, gender, and creed posed challenges, race introduced a more complex set of issues for higher education beginning in the mid-1800s. Issues grew more critical with the potential for social equality and miscegenation made possible when blacks and whites were present on the same campuses. The second Morrill Act of 1890 provided for separate but equal education for black students at institutions in seventeen southern states (land grant historically black colleges and universities). However, the U.S. Supreme Court decision rendered in *Brown* v. *Topeka Board of Education* in 1954 noted that these and other educational institutions provided separate education that was not on an equal footing with similar predominantly white institutions. Despite legislation, minority groups still sensed a feeling or noted substantial proof that levels of accessibility and inclusiveness were still lacking (Wechsler, 1997).

Faculty Versus Administration

As student numbers grew, faculty moved, often physically and philosophically, from more general supervisory duties to a faculty role and remanded business matters and student oversight to administrative personnel. They could seek prestige on campus or seek it nationally through speaking, publishing, consulting, and involvement with professional organizations. Discontent with university administration and university governance broadened this chasm and created more faculty isolation, which has become characteristic of the twentieth-century professoriat (Veysey, 1965).

Because the development of the American university followed more of the industrial model, governance appeared hierarchical. The hierarchical bureaucratic model contributed to miscommunication and increased the opportunity for mounting distrust between faculty and administration (Boyer, 1997; Kerr, 1982). Historically, faculty rights to academic freedom were challenged by legislation and the general public through the 1960s and 1970s. Faculty sought protection through unionizing. Attempts to unionize delineated the chasm between faculty and administration as well as between pro-union advocates and nonunion conservatives. Unionized universities and colleges during contract negotiations have been notorious for uncivil action and retaliation (Ruger & Bickel, 2004).

Faculty guild as corporation has evolved more into the administration as corporation, as administrators seem to be forced to search for ways to attract market share. This shift in philosophy and mission rendered the system of higher education more businesslike and its faculty members often more concerned for their personal well-being, to the detriment of the traditional mission aimed at the public good (Slaughter, Archerd, & Campbell, 2004). As a result, the university notion of wanting to be all things to all people, though admirable, poses the problem of mission creep—that is, straying from core values such as teaching and service (Scott, 2006) in favor of market share.

Perhaps one of the new tensions introduced in higher education with the advent of women on campus was their repeated contact with a glass ceiling that prevented them from gaining leadership positions. The networks employed by male counterparts to move upward through the organization did not acknowledge the same movement by new and different populations of faculty. Shavlik and Touchton (1984) argued that one group advanced on potential (male faculty), while the other group had to demonstrate proven ability in order to advance (female faculty).

Liberal Arts Curriculum Versus Vocationalism

Sparks between liberal arts faculty and vocational/professional faculty continue to smolder. A decline of student interest in liberal arts fields eroded the need for full-time liberal arts faculty while also triggering conflict between them and faculty teaching in professional and vocational areas as students have shifted to more applied or vocationally oriented programs (Morphew & Hartley, 2006).

Historical shifts in higher education have moved from industrial models where vocational training was an outcome of the postindustrial/information/technological era. Vocation has evolved into professional education. While some would argue that nothing much has changed, others would conclude there is a somewhat elitist tone in the name change from *vocational* to *professional*. Specialized education has been valued over more general curriculums because those specialized fields have gained legitimacy and prominence through certificate- or licensure-driven outcomes (Grubb & Lazerson, 2005). The result is that "students can exchange a degree for professional status" rather than obtain a well-rounded, liberal arts education (p. 9). Professional program faculty may not argue for a liberal, well-rounded education. Their reason is concern for coverage of material that will likely appear on board examinations that students must pass for licensure. Higher student passage rates translate to a more competitive advantage for prospective students by the institution.

While both faculty groups provide strong arguments for their respective curriculums, there will always be an argument for the presence of liberal arts courses in the curriculum. The reason is not so much for the greater good of humanity but to ensure that liberal arts faculties have something to teach, thus sustaining their jobs. Although professional and liberal arts faculty will continue to snub one another based on their curricular stance in the academy,the reality is that the demand for their knowledge now rests with the student as consumer.

Cosmopolitans Versus Locals

Damrosch (1995) recalled a stagnant period, between 1965 and 1995, when the university was unable to reconstruct academic life to address change. He noted that faculty did not behave like good citizens but rather more like resident aliens. Collegiality on campus was becoming rarer, interdisciplinary and intradisciplinary work was being bypassed, and each area had developed a distinct ethos that deviated slightly from its first cousins. Given that academe had typically been isolated and individualistic, the effect of poor citizenry reverberated through academic departments and divisions. Departments acted more like families with patriarchs at the top: paternalism was assumed, and judgment and evaluation were expected. As the same time, research faculty were seeking free agency through their research and professional association, trying to avoid the campus academic "family." Damrosch referred to the phenomenon as the "politics of specialization" (p. 57).

The adaptation of the German research model to the American liberal arts institution served as well to separate faculty members with campus allegiance (locals) from those faculty members doing research. The latter group focused their efforts on and loyalty to their academic specialization (cosmopolitans) rather than to the institution, which is what the former group valued (Boyer, 1997; Gouldner, 1957, 1958; Kerr, 1982).

According to Rosenzweig (1998), those academics conducting high-quality research believed they were richly deserving of more resources despite the subsequent shortfall of those resources. Those who had always received research dividends continued to believe in their Midas touch.

Faculty members became more socialized and professionalized after World War II, ultimately increasing their physical isolation on campus while strengthening their research status and national reputation. This enhanced colleagues' reputations in their respective professional associations. While these learned societies amassed their own political influence on national policy, the campus professoriat needed its own protection. The distinctions between cosmopolitans and locals widened (Gouldner, 1957, 1958).

Rosenzweig (1998) noted that more money was available in the 1970s and 1980s for research, which made the pursuit for money more advantageous for faculty. Grants and business and industry investments painted a rosy picture for faculty researchers, that is, a promise for the future. Because all parties were rewarded in the grant, it was logical that the universities would move in the direction of rewarding faculty members who did research. But university missions still indicated teaching before research, although concomitant merit pay and other rewards associated with tenure and promotion were likely to reward research success. Rosenzweig lamented, "Prosperity thus carried with it the seeds of bitterness and conflict that would flower in later decades" (p. 7). He recalled that the turmoil of the 1960s decreased civility, causing presidential turnovers, low public confidence in academics, campus protests, and challenges to and suspicions of sponsored research.

Competition for research funding from business and industry increased as a result of the 1980 Bayh-Dole Act, which pitted business norms of selling research outcomes to the highest bidder against the older, traditional value of university research, that is, research on which further research is built (Rozenzweig, 1998; Slaughter, Archerd, & Campbell, 2004). Legislators promoted economic growth with the university as the foundation for national growth patterns. Funding bypassed the merits of research for its own sake in exchange for researcher monetary gain. This raised conflict among faculty. Not only had teaching faculty been alienated by colleagues focused on research, but now the research faculty were split as to why they conducted research in the first place, that is, for public good or private benefit.

Gouldner's notions of cosmopolitan and local (1957, 1958) described the internal tension between individual faculty who must choose between loyalty to their profession or discipline and loyalty to their institution. This extended to tension between colleagues who were in the same department but did not share similar sentiments with regard to professional specialty or organizational policy and politics (Altbach, 1995). This produced fertile ground for continued tension between faculties and challenged the notion of collegiality.

While Damrosch (1995) acknowledged that faculty own the means of production and knowledge is their product, he added that unlike other businesses and industry, faculty in their departments rarely work together to produce that product, be it through team teaching, co-administrative situations, or exclusively collaborative research. Furthermore, those who produced knowledge also disseminated it. These faculty producers raised additional funding to add value to their original products, making it an unlinked, uncoordinated process between campus disciplinary divisions. Knowledge production can also come from or be enhanced by grants, course releases, and other rewards. For instance, if a junior professor works at a university that links successful grant writing with tenure and promotion and the government is offering grants to women researching minority children in STEM (science, engineering, technology, and math) fields, she might write for and research an applicable topic, but it may not be a primary area of her interest or her department's. In other words, cosmopolitan opportunities may not interconnect with local interests. The push for tenure and the staple of peer review also caused consternation with the administrative push for these grants to offset costs related to research agendas or something else. In this instance, the administration would be pleased, but the research might do little to poise the junior faculty candidate for tenure in the estimation of peers in an engineering department, for instance.

Damrosch (1995) posited that the modern university has a foundation of "alienation and aggression" (p. 78). To illustrate, a group researching to address social ills as an end in itself looks and acts differently from one focused on researching as a means to an end, that is, to get tenure, incorporate a start-up company, or compete for consulting opportunities. Both groups are present on university faculties. Damrosch acknowledged that "aggression directed against other scholars, has always had an important role to play in scholarly debate" (p. 82). This behavior can be positive and absorbed and tolerated in the name of intellectual advancement, academic freedom, or societal improvement. However, the shift in the economic-entrepreneur-corporate modality renders such competition and scholarly aggression little different from street corner violence. He added that "alienation breeds a defensive aggressiveness [which] magnifies that alienation" (p. 96). The result can be detrimental.

Academic Freedom Versus Paternalism

Dating back to 1940, the American Association of University Professors (AAUP) Statement on Principles of Academic Freedom and Tenure noted that autonomy, academic freedom, promotion and tenure, basic treatment by administrators, and inclusion in campus decision making were subject to normative standards across campuses. Faculty seeking grievance could be assured that their cases would be similarly investigated. With the thrust of the

AAUP, individual campus policies could be modified to a more standard level and ensure faculty representation in governance (Freeland, 1997). This was a banner day for faculty. However, attacks on and investigations of faculty during the McCarthy witch hunts of the 1950s pitted colleague against colleague. For one thing, the interpretation of what is or what is not academic freedom was called into question (Hutcheson, 1997). Little did higher education realize that suspicion of old guard faculty for newer entering groups was just beginning to simmer.

The establishment of women's studies programs in the academy challenged male dominance and dominant male values in the prevailing academic culture. Unfortunately, given the governance structure, these programs were marginalized and lacked real power. Male-centered governance and curriculum were sustained and maintained, making it difficult for women's studies programs to gain parity in the academy, especially economic parity in terms of rewards and basic resources. Some of these university programs starved financially as a result of political manipulation (Burghardt & Colbeck, 2005). Perhaps the most important finding in their study of twenty women in four prominent women's studies programs is that in order for these women to achieve promotion and tenure, they had to conform to institutional normative standards rather than pursue research agendas that supported feminist scholarship.

Academe Versus Academics

Historically, what academics do and have done in the past 150 years has changed very little. Academics still struggle to balance teaching, research, and service. However, what has occurred is a response to that imposed change as to how faculty view their relationship and responsibility to the university and to each other. In his discussion of the rise of academic faculty professionalization, Finkelstein (1997) alluded to multiple instances where strides in faculty role development and orientation had to "await an institutional structure within which to operate" (p. 31). It appears now that the organizational structure has made the necessary changes but awaits the faculty to adopt or adjust to it. What is difficult for faculty to accept is that faculty, not the administration or the student consumers, apparently have usually dictated the change.

Finally, Robbins and Kahn (1985) noted the irony of incivility in an academic "community that prides itself on its principled standards and values" (p. 8). Academics "are the perpetrators as well as the victims, the people who deny that discrimination exists as well as those who experience and document it" (p. 8). Young (1978) labeled "subjective judgments in professional and academic settings" as the culprit (p. 43); thus, we inhibit our own progress, the very thing that faculty and knowledge creation are. Damrosch (1995) traced evidence in academe as "a disunity of inquiry," where unity and collaboration were to exist in the modern university but rarely do. He wrote about how the university reflected society, ironically, "both opposing it and mirroring it, even reproducing many of the features it most wished to oppose" (p. 37). Throughout the history of higher education in America, one of those features has been incivility despite its pretense toward the contrary. In the next chapter, we look at underlying theory that explains reasons for persons to be uncivil and bully.

3

Learning Incivility

*Man's deepest impulses are bad, evil, undesirable,
selfish, criminal, or otherwise reprehensible.*

Abraham Maslow

How do we learn to be uncivil and to bully others? Sociology, anthropology, social psychology, and social learning theory deal with individual behavior patterns framed in social context. Aggression and the biosocial side of human nature, including manifestations of power, paternalism, and competition in the academic workplace, factor into the equation. Dziech and Weiner (1990) acknowledged power differentials and the misuse of power as displaying "unhealthy . . . dynamics [and behaviors] that are exploitative, abusive, and psychologically . . . damaging" (p. 25). We asked our participants to identify the perpetrators of incivility and bullying. The list was exhaustive, encompassing junior and senior faculty colleagues, students in class, and all levels of staff or line administrators. Their victims included junior and senior faculty, administrative assistants, and secretaries. George, one of the participants, reiterated, "Not all . . . just a few . . . it doesn't take many."

Social Learning Theory and the Rise of Aggression

Aggression increases naturally as the population increases. When humans are brought closer to one another but still expect the "smooth functioning of intricate interdependent systems" (Bandura, 1973, p. 1), aggression is likely to occur. For Maslow (1949) and Montagu (1956), aggression is a result of frustration. Maslow said, "Man's deepest impulses are bad, evil, undesirable, selfish, criminal, or otherwise reprehensible" (p. 273). Aggression, or what Maslow thought was instinctive animal behavior, is more learned than instinctive. He concurred with other social psychologists that the connection between this emotion and response is cultural. Frustration can manifest itself in aggression if the culture has socialized its members to elicit such response. Through social learning theory, Bandura indicated we distinguish which acts constitute aggression and which do not.

Montagu (1956) called aggression "the overt expression of a feeling of hostility and the function of the overt act is to inflict injury upon the object towards which hostility is felt" (p. 58). Aggression can cause physical as well as psychological harm. In their research, Jennifer, Cowie, and Ananiadou (2003) found that aggressors pose persistent threats to their colleagues' personal or professional status, cause professional isolation, and undermine colleagues' work.

Bandura (1973) acknowledged that social learning takes place deliberately by inadvertently observing others as well as through direct personal experience. How each of us internalizes that learning comes from cues or responses as well as the degree and presence of reinforcement following the response. Social circumstances therefore determine behavior, including aggressive behavior. These circumstances can be from direct modeling of the behavior of others or gained indirectly from watching such behavior unobtrusively and noting that it goes unpunished. These aggressive behaviors can be isolated instances or serial experiences over an extended period of time. The latter implies that perhaps people who were victims of incivility or bullied as children are likely to become adult bullies (Henry, 2004). Furthermore, if their behaviors are reinforced, bullies repeat these successful, though negative, acts (Rayner, Hoel, & Cooper, 2002). According to Skinner (1953), if positive reinforcement or no negative reinforcement follows the actor, behaviors are deemed appropriate to repeat. Thus, bullies become effective social learners.

According to Bandura (1973), "Aggressive actions tend to occur at certain times, in certain settings, toward certain objects or individuals, and in response to certain forms of provocation" (p. 115). If we see someone else acting a certain way, we will likely follow especially if we assume there will be rewards and no punishments. To act in prescribed ways within one's culture presumes the act has "proven functional value" (p. 115). The acts become performance cues for others. Ultimately people are more likely to follow the performance cues of those with social power or social status within an organization. When others see the responses to those acts are either approval or unpunished indifference, the likelihood of subsequent performances is probable.

When I was on leave a second time, the adjunct who used my office trashed it, took my name off the door . . . changed my phone message to his. I told him to replace my name, return the office the way he found it, use it, put his name alongside mine. When I returned, I confronted the adjunct and asked him why. He said the chair told him he could do it. But I asked him not to. He said, again, that he could. I took back my keys and told him I hope she [the chair] is still beholden to you because I'm not going to do anything to help you adjunct here anymore. — Ben

I have seen bullies get spots on prestigious committees, be offered special positions with extra monies associated with them, be highlighted in institutional publications for their great work, and all because they were able to bully themselves into positions that deceptively make them look good or others look bad. — Kathy

---

Ensuring conformity to organizational goals by pressuring others to alter their existing behaviors to align with what they see, hear, and perceive may call for uncivil action or bullying (Ironside & Seifert, 2003). Aggressive behavior that is legitimized through approval or indifference will be replicated and eventually inculcated because the risk of punishment is low or nonexistent. The uncivil behavior becomes more self-regulated and normative. This does not imply that all people will suddenly see the value of aggressiveness and incivility and participate. It does, however, imply that their inhibition or predisposition to it is more relaxed. Bandura (1973) offered instances where the possibility is greater: "People experience different outcomes for aggressing toward individuals who differ in status, power, age, sex, and many other attributes . . . [and] therefore attack not only those whom they have learned to dislike, but also those whom it is relatively safe to attack and those whom it is advantageous to attack" (p. 136).

The program director and his sidekick blame the chair for anything that is bad/was bad. They take no responsibility or blame. They blame her [the department chair] for everything that is wrong. She supported him [the program director] and he has no loyalty to her, only himself. — Ben

---

When victimization occurs along the academic career path appears to have some bearing on the nature of incivility, bullying, or mobbing. For instance, faculty on a career path toward tenure and/or promotion are likely to feel and react more strongly to uncivil or bullying acts the closer they are to the tenure decision. They may be more sensitive to the actions and reactions of colleagues, especially those on the promotion and tenure committee. Trower, Austin, and Sorcinelli (2001) reported that pretenure faculty recall instances of isolation and incivility during their early years in a department. The more passionate or invested and involved a faculty member is with specific activities may cause them to intensify the perception of an act as civil or uncivil (Thomas, 1923). In other words, an untenured faculty member may be more susceptible to discussions about his or her work, perceiving them as gossip, when in fact it may be a legitimate assessment of his or her credentials. By the same token, if that discussion also includes personal or philosophical differences, it probably is gossip and thus inappropriate to the value placed on the credential file alone. If the latter discussion falls so close to a tenure committee meeting and tenure is denied, logically the candidate assumes denial was based on the gossip and perhaps other committee members were swayed toward that denial as a direct result of the gossip.

I started crying when this colleague who had been on a tirade [because she claimed I did not do a quick enough turnaround on the work she assigned to me] left my office and I literally could not stop crying throughout the subsequent faculty meeting. I sat in the back of the room with my head down, and the tears just flowed. The humiliation of it all was traumatic for me. While it was the end of the encounter for her, it made me incredibly cautious, not willing to do more work than was absolutely necessary. It made me realize that people didn't know the volume of work I had. So I spent more of my time self-promoting, telling people what I was doing. I don't advertise what I do, but people needed to realize I am overworked . . . see things they never see . . . my time is encumbered. — Lucille

---

Goffman (1959) acknowledged that actors in the workplace allow some roles to be revealed and others concealed. Some roles are more seamless, but the faculty member must be in control of appropriate presentations of self in some consistent fashion with each performance of his or her role no matter how mismatched the roles may be. For example, a faculty member could simultaneously be professor, adviser, conference organizer, peer reviewer, mentor, scholar, committee chair, dissertation chair, and bully. Masterful aggressors can use their social network and role opportunities to indirectly express anger and incivility by taking a circuitous route to conceal their behaviors so as not to be detected or linked back to the aggression or the victim (Heim & Murphy, 2001).

During my appeals process, I was tied up in knots, nerves frayed. During a faculty meeting, the one male colleague who orchestrated the nonrenewal of my contract said how wonderfully professional I was. He said I had received wonderful feedback from students. And you just eat it and smile. Perhaps, if I had done that [instead of challenging], I would have been more successful, but I didn't pick up on the cue. — Caroline

---

Social Learning and Gender

Male universal dominance exists (Goldberg, 1973). Males are aggressive by biological makeup and concomitantly socialized as such as part of their biosocial nature. Women are neither biologically built nor culturally socialized for such aggression, nor is it part of women's biosocial nature. Men seek out opportunities to be dominant and authoritative, and bureaucracies provide that opportunity. Women have not been socialized to seek out dominant positions. However, when women attempt to gain equality, men seek out other opportunities to be authoritative. As women gradually take hold of academe, traditionally a male stronghold, men, according to Goldberg, will seek ways to reassert their dominance because in nature, patriarchy is inevitable. One way to accomplish that has been through workplace aggression.

When a woman was chosen as dean, several of the men in the division set up every possible roadblock in her effort to be successful. There was a man they wanted as dean and did not quit bullying the female until she left the position and the man got it. To this day, some people still talk about those days, saying derogatory things about her term of office. I always ask if they have that information firsthand and if it is some gossip someone told them. More often than not, they are repeating what someone told them, not the reality, which was that she did what needed to be done to run the college. — Kathy

Chesler (1972) noted that American children are socialized for competition but also expected to get along with one another. She posited that most people will repress individual acts of aggression and opt for conformity for fear of ostracism.

Men may use the organizational system to bully others, while women have been socialized not to be aggressive and thus use a more sugar-coated passive approach. Women's overt aggression would be determined garish and socially unacceptable, but covert aggression proves to be a more socially acceptable approach. Thus, women are better able to manipulate a person or situation through indirect, passive-aggressive means.

To be more socially appropriate, women engage in gossip as an acceptable feminine form of power and aggression, but the repercussions of that gossip for the unsuspecting recipient are no less deadly than a direct physical or verbal blow (Heim & Murphy, 2001).

When I came, I had a mentor — a senior woman. At some point, she turned against me, but in a very quiet way. I did not see it coming. She was becoming more distant, but I just passed it off. Nobody told us anything; we had to figure it out for ourselves. I kept asking my mentor for help in dealing with an evening class of graduate students who were clearly indignant to me *during* class. But she clearly was not going to back me up on anything. I found out later that my mentor actually orchestrated the behavior of the class. She really didn't like me, and my politics and my course readings were from a critical theory perspective, and she felt there was no place for that in the classroom. I subsequently asked another faculty member for help. She never had time for me. Then later she said I never asked her for help. She lied to me. I tried to step back and intellectualize what had happened through the whole ordeal. . . . I told a colleague that I should have seen this coming. — Caroline

I did not really understand passive-aggressive behavior until I witnessed it in my division. Several of us were appointed to a committee to make some curricular changes with regard to courses we commonly taught. This happened several times over a period of about three years. Although this one particular woman was considered an expert in the area of the proposed changes, she made very few contributions to the cause. It took me awhile to figure this out. She allowed her name to appear on the committee rosters but did not contribute because she was not in favor of the changes. This way, if no one commented on her lack of contributions, she was able to get by with appearing to be cooperative but in reallty providing obstacles all along the way. Eventually I learned to recognize this as passive-aggressive behavior. — Kathy

---

Social Learning, Social Distance, and Paternalism

Bandura (1973) built on Leon Festinger's (1954) social comparison theory to explain that people in similar social situations naturally compare themselves to their peers. Becker and Carper (1966) noted in their comparative study of humanities and science professionals that these groups compared themselves "to those upon whom their success in [that] institution depend[ed]" (p. 105). In achieving tenure in academe, junior professors must comply with the expectations of senior colleagues who have penned the tenure document and sit on the tenure committee. In order to accomplish tenure, junior faculty might compare their work to the standard set by those already tenured and emulate that path to tenure, bowing, if need be, to departmental expectations.

Reynolds (1992) distinguished between socialization and acculturation into one's department. If the junior professor's view of the departmental norms was similar to his or her own, then it became easier for the new faculty member to become socialized into these normative patterns. If the new faculty member's social interdependence differed from the prevailing departmental norms, then this junior professor would have to change his or her behavior patterns by undergoing an acculturation process that could mean value as well as behavior changes in order to remain in that department and seek tenure and promotion. Otherwise the faculty member could be subjected to isolation from colleagues. If junior faculty take note of the disparity and incongruence that serve to widen the gap between socially acceptable and unacceptable behavior, they may open a door to victimization because the target is viewed as a dissenter, agitator, or ingrate. The ambiguity and mystique that often surround the tenure process provide a fertile ground for insecurity, suspicion, and rumor. How junior faculty manage the journey to tenure may be closely monitored unobtrusively, ardently, or visibly by others depending on how senior faculty feels about tenuring that person.

The classic Milgram (1963) experiments of the 1960s showed the effects of social and ecological distance between perpetrator and victim with regard to a perpetrator's ability to inflict pain on a victim. Purposefully using deception in his experiment, Milgram determined the inverse relationship between imposed action and the degree of personalization. In other words, the more removed the perpetrator is from the victim, the easier it becomes to administer pain. Contrarily, such action is more difficult to administer the more personalized the circumstances. Hence, bullying inflicted in committee proceedings is more easily administered than face-to-face.

Because of this, groups such as tenure committees provide safe havens for bullies, who can say what they want within the confines of the committee, supposedly without fear that the candidate in question will ever know how the bully really feels. We say "supposedly," of course, because this contention rests on the premise that the bully will not betray the confidence of the committee. We know, however, that that may well not be true. And if in fact the bully does betray the confidence, he or she is likely to make himself or herself sound like the savior and condemn the other committee members.

Social distance may be translated to discipline-specific issues and become part of the socialization process. In his exploratory study comparing departments in the hard and soft disciplines, Slawski (1973) hypothesized that faculty and students in the harder sciences encounter greater social and ecological distance from one another. By contrast, those in the softer social sciences had greater social closeness, to the point of being cliquish. He learned that while this sounded positive, clique behavior could be counterproductive and lead to exclusion of nonclique members. Katz (2006) admonished that because the faculty "have so little loyalty to our particular university, we are less likely to serve it well, either in the classroom or in the performance of other necessary functions" (p. B9). Because each profession or discipline transports us as individuals to our own unique niche or specialization, we as professors are less and less alike and share fewer basic commonalities. This serves only to broaden the chasms we discussed in Chapter Two. As this social distance increases, we are seeing less collegiality and more incivility.

Academe traditionally has been patriarchic and paternalistic (Goldberg, 1973). However, acts of seemingly innocuous paternalism could result in subsequent action that stands to victimize unsuspecting academic colleagues. The bully or aggressor is likely shielded from individual ownership of such action because these behaviors have become acceptable. These paternalistic actions have become deeply engrained in academe. Paternalistic actions are regarded as normative especially because they appear to be nonconfrontational; in fact, they appear to be exactly the opposite. These behaviors manifest themselves as acts of kindness; the bully appears to be assisting or helping an unsuspecting colleague. However, paternalistic behaviors are camouflaged in statements like, "The committee wants what is best for you" or "The committee is operating in the best interest of the candidate." These types of individual- or committee-generated responses may not be reported because this type of behavior is often accepted as normative (Ferris, 2004; Miller, 1986; Olaffson & Johannsdottir, 2004).

On an individual level, this paternalism often translates into indebtedness. Before he recognizes the behavior for what it is, the bullied colleague is in debt to the bully; he or she owes the bully something and will surely find out what that payment is in the future.

Power and Politics

De Waal (2005), in characterizing power, indicated that we try to cover our motives for wielding power even though we all have power and the potential to wield it. Weiner (2002) identified bullies as self-centered, power-hungry workers who are territorial, desiring status, highly competitive, challenged by others, and pushed to extremes by a survival-of-the-fittest mentality. Bullies are shameless because they target weaker individuals as a way to overcome their own inadequacy (Namie & Namie, 2003).

When I went up for full [professor], the female chair wrote a beautiful two-and-a-half-page letter of support for me. Because I took a leave, I did not proceed further until I returned. While I was gone, she changed. This time she wrote a half-page letter downing me. People in the department united while I was gone because she was doing nasty things. When asked why she did them, she responded, "Because I can. What can you do about it?" She became powerless because of the program director and his buddy. She had a weak personality to begin with, and she was angry. She probably felt abandoned by me when I left for a year. When the chair's term expired, she was replaced by the VP because no one in the department wanted to be chair. The VP saw the discrepancy in the two letters. The P&T [promotion and tenure] committee called her in for an interview when they saw them. I got promoted. The committee confronted the bully. — Ben

Given adverse circumstances, faculty jockey for power. They use micropolitics to improve their status or increase their power base. In fact, to increase social, cultural, or political capital in academe is regarded as normative and acceptable, and it is often encouraged. As a result, incivility might go unnoticed and likely be attributed to self-promotion. In other words, traditional culture actually excuses some degree of incivility and explains it away as the quest for advancement and name recognition. This passive acceptance of incivility becomes inadvertently tolerated and even rewarded (Brodsky, 1976; Zapf & Einarsen, 2003).

To be successful as a bully often requires an entourage—a bevy of believers, that is, witting or unwitting allies who are part of a powerful elite. Bullies seek out powerful allies to tack on to their legitimate position power (French & Raven, 1960). Bully personalities are also likely to seek power positions, ally themselves with powerful people, or offer criticism of others in power positions, hoping one day to replace them.

Colleagues treated a female dean as though she had committed a grievous offense by accepting the position when offered to her. The folks who wanted the in-house male candidate rallied around him to make life miserable for the new dean. It was never clear to me, however, that the in-house candidate contributed to the incivility. Some might say he did not have to; his allies were taking care of it. It also might be the case that he didn't even realize what they were doing on his behalf. — Kathy

Some people are oblivious to their ability to bully, others derive pleasure from it, and the remainder could not care less what havoc they wreak on others by their bullying (Braithwaite, 2001). When the uncivil behavior is reinforced, the bully assumes an invulnerable persona. This legitimizes the bully behavior, setting the bully above criticism. Challenging the bully often means taking on a powerful mob or challenging the system (Namie & Namie, 2003).

To the elite, the mob, the administration, or the newcomer, the bully may be an accomplished charmer or has some human or social capital that has totem, or exchange, value in their academic marketplace. Braithwaite (2001) labeled these charmers "liars" who conjure up or manipulate the truth to suit their own circumstances. Bullying tends to thrive in workplaces where competition and jealously linger.

When the graduate course listings come out, if a TBA [to be announced] is beside a class, we get dibs on them before adjuncts. Of course, 90 percent of the courses are spoken for. I sent an e-mail to the program director and blind-carbon-copied it to the VP, asking for a particular course. I had my spouse do the same with another course. This program director rejects my wife's request, but I don't hear back. When I asked him, he said, "I asked you to see me, and

you didn't, so I gave it to someone else." I said it was an outright lie
and "I challenge you to get IT [information technology] to look into the
computer to show that you sent such a letter and I received it." He
replied to just "sit tight." I wanted to see if the blacklisting would still
go on and if the program director would continue to insubordinate
the VP when I asked for the TBA course. I wanted to provoke the
bully. I know I will never teach a grad course here again. — Ben

---

Bandura (1973) acknowledged the work of Milgram (1963) to illustrate that those in positions of legitimate authority have the power (French & Raven, 1960; Weber, 1948) to instigate, condone, and support uncivil behavior. Furthermore, collective action powerfully controls uncivil individuals in that people go along with group decisions regardless of how misguided they are (Westhues, 2005) and acknowledge the power of the group in the same way they acknowledge a singular legitimate authority. Perpetrators believe group action is the rational excuse for the behavior rather than attributing one's individual choice as cause for the uncivil behavior (Bandura, 1973; Milgram, 1963).

Dziech and Weiner (1990) illustrated that besides the obvious legitimate power that faculty hold as a result of status and rank, they hold individual referent and expert power (French & Raven, 1960). In other words, people want to be like them, follow them, and marvel at and seek out their expertise. These types of nonposition power imply freedom from constraint as a result of increased personal autonomy on the job. These powers are associated with breadth and depth of faculty knowledge and accomplishment (Altbach & Finkelstein, 1997). Academic freedom and autonomy extend to faculty teaching and service behaviors as well as research interests. For some faculty, these freedoms lead to self-confidence, self-aggrandizement, heightened self-image, pomposity, and sometimes the perception of untouchability. The charisma associated with referent power and special knowledge common to expert power holders can be exhilarating to its users and intoxicating to their followers (French & Raven, 1960). Thus, the professoriat can become a protected sanctuary. This sanctuary can accommodate a range of scholars and researchers, from Mr. Chips to Dr. Frankenstein. Protecting academic freedom and autonomy is paramount to the professoriat given the struggle to achieve these sacred privileges and protections in the first place. Fighting to keep them is understandable, but in this ego-centered academic environment, it tempts arrogance (Dziech & Weiner, 1990). Arrogance might allow one person or group to dress down another in order to show some professional or character defect. By the same token, it could also signal one's inability to cope with matters and lash out. Incivility could arise from either situation.

Heim and Murphy (2001) remind us that power is in the perception of the receiver or perceiver, not the wielder, which means there is considerable room for misperception of power levels or power differentials. This has implications for gender, as men and women learn to deal with power differently. For instance, men might be swayed more by the symbolic nature of the spoils of bullying as well as by the thrill of wielding symbolic power. Women are not used to or adept at either; instead, they are more likely than men to be jealous of the symbols and trappings of power and do what they perceive will render them more powerful.

When I realized what was going on, I asked one female colleague how she had put up with it so long, and she said she went into her office and wrote to get tenure. She still wrote, but now it was for pleasure. The men are still going to do what they are going to do, and there is nothing that she could do about it, so she said she just writes. — Caroline

---

Males are more likely than women to blame others or seek fault in others; females are more likely to blame themselves or perhaps displace their frustrations on someone else. As a result, females can be critical of one another, especially other women, if they experience a power differential. Women are prone to gossip about other women and judge behavior more critically than men do. Heim and Murphy (2001) would argue that women can be their own worst critics rather than supporting one another's victories. They may resort to indirect means such as infighting and sabotage. These researchers hold that both men and women have the potential to be uncivil, but the motivations behind and the manifestations of their uncivil behavior differ. In fact, while aggressors are typically males more so than females, any-place where persons serve in a superordinate, managerial, or power capacity over colleagues or subordinates can set the stage for incivility and bullying (Hoel, Einarsen, & Cooper, 2003; Zapf & Einarsen, 2003).

Aggressive Behavior and Management Styles

Workplace incivility, bullying, and aggressive behaviors may be linked to specific types of management styles. For instance, employees' acceptance of an autocratic management style from supervisors may inadvertently mask workplace aggression (Ferris, 2004; McCarthy & Mayhew, 2004; Rayner, Hoel, & Cooper, 2002). Much bullying has been reported in business and industry because of the superordinate-subordinate relationship of workers. Historically, academe functions on more of a flattened governance structure, but that has changed since the late 1980s.

A laissez-faire type of supervisor might be prone to avoid dealing with workplace aggressive behavior (Hoel & Salin, 2003). It is possible that residual behaviors stemming from an acceptable autocratic management style could legitimately harbor and support acts of administrative bullying. For instance, disproportionate work overloads assigned by an autocratic administrator or supervisor are possible. So too is unwarranted criticism from management (Olaffson & Johannsdottir, 2004). These recurrent intentional behaviors by a superior could likely cause supervisees humiliation, offense, or distress (Einarsen, 1999). Both the supervisor and the victim might presume that these bullying behaviors are typical, necessary, warranted, commonplace, and acceptable.

By contrast, the common academic laissez-faire management style of a department chair that may be highly valued by faculty could prove detrimental to individual faculty who are bullied within that department. Under this management style, a bully finds easy targets among colleagues because he or she perceives that the administrator will not know what is happening or have the wherewithal to cope. Unfortunately for the bullied victims, redress through administrative channels can be difficult because there is no support or insufficient support from the chair and perhaps other department colleagues (Peyton, 2003; Rayner, Hoel, & Cooper, 2002).

Since this incident [my colleague accused me of not doing the work she had asked me to do as quickly as she expected it] happened to me, I have been so cautious. Three years after it happened, I realized that from all appearances, this person looked like a friend. There were other strengths this person had that I appreciated later, but it was always with great caution that I interacted with her. I learned later she treated other people that way. Another colleague later brought up that the faculty member yelled at them, and I said, "Really?" This person opened up, and I said that I had had a similar experience. It really traumatized me. — Lucille

When the VP became chair of our department, he made every attempt to get us to restructure ourselves. He made teams. The minute he misses a meeting, the program director and sidekick act miserably to me. At one meeting, the program director made an outright attack at me in front of the VP. I didn't say a word. The VP told him to calm down. — Ben

---

With academic governance functioning through committees, governance processes have the potential to conceal passive-aggressive behaviors through groupthink or mobbing practices (Janis, 1982, 1988; Westhues, 2005). Administrators may not be aware of what is going on because they are typically not present for certain types of faculty meetings. Bullies may be astute enough to avoid uncivil actions during departmental meetings where administrators would likely be able to witness them. The committee is the perfect place to camouflage the action because its members will wittingly or unwittingly assume the burden for the uncivil actions of the bully and his or her allies. Furthermore, the likelihood of challenging those actions successfully is minuscule. This shows that it is difficult to separate the bully, mob, or uncivil action from the context of the organizational structure.

Competitiveness and Domination

Academic life is competitive. Finkelstein, Seal, and Schuster (1998) noted the constant battle for dominance among institutions, academic programs, athletic programs, academic journals, fields of study, and individual faculty. Becher and Trowler (2001) claimed that faculty reputation is paramount, so individual faculty compete for position, space in top-tier journals, finite grant monies, best-developed theory, most cited in journals (not counting when you cite yourself), most publications per year, highest-paying consulting positions, most keynote addresses given at international conferences, brightest doctoral students, closest parking space, biggest office with a window, most golden in the dean's eyes, and most prestigious endowed chair. While institutions and university faculty may value, reward, and welcome collaboration with colleagues and students, a professional reputation is gained in singular fashion through a research agenda, perhaps of first or singularly authored publications in prestigious journals.

Teaching has also remained predominantly a singular activity despite sporadic team teaching and pushes for collaborative scholarship (Boyer, 1990). Academic life moves in many ways through passion: passion for one's subject matter or one's research, passion for an underserved group to be researched and heard, passion for training subsequent generations of scholars. While passion is presented as individualistic and positive, pursuit of these passions can take numerous avenues, both positive and negative (Becher & Trowler, 2001). The argument follows that if someone gets in the way of another's passion, the competition heats up, and incivility likely follows.

According to Blackburn and Lawrence (1995), "Today's more competitive academic environment endangers a faculty member's chances for success" (p. 215). National recognition of one's work comes from research and scholarship much more so than efforts at stellar pedagogy. Teaching is more individual and local and thus is less likely to be seen or revered nationally. In contrast, research and scholarship are intended for the cosmopolitan audience. For most professors, pedagogical information is not likely to extend far beyond the classroom or the semester, a situation that socializes most faculties to develop a greater loyalty to their profession and their scholarly pursuits than to their institution (Gouldner, 1957, 1958). This is especially true of research universities.

Very few people are aware of a faculty member's reputation on his or her own campus. However, off-campus colleagues will know of that person's research and publications. To gain any sense of notoriety not readily available on campus or in the department, faculty attend conferences and present, and perhaps invest themselves in professional organizations through our service

(Twale & Shannon, 1996). In any case, there is a tendency to overlook how a scholar got to an exalted reputation, because the recognition goes only to the most recent published accomplishment (Blackburn & Lawrence, 1995). Competition for dominance may be more than academic dominance because it may come at the expense of incivility to fellow faculty. Faculty, departments, and divisions have the potential to harbor aggression by varying degrees and in isolated pockets across any institution (White, 2004).

Struggles within the department, with colleagues, with administration, and with students remain largely unknown to outsiders. In fact, some faculty may reach the status of urban legend. The value of one's credentials may be so inflated by the faculty member or by the administration, for instance, that his or her students or colleagues from another school on campus may believe that this faculty walks on water and thus gains a legendary reputation among them that is more pomposity and pretense than actual value and substance. Peers off campus who know about the person's work through presentation at conferences are more likely to provide a truer assessment of the credentials. However, a journal, book, or textbook consumer may never know that the coveted author whose work they read and long to meet acts uncivilly to colleagues or passive-aggressively maneuvers promotion decisions. That reputation seldom extends beyond the campus perimeter or perhaps beyond the committee, department, or college.

With the fierce competition for space in journals, not to mention top-tier journals, expectations exist for a high caliber of research (Blackburn & Lawrence, 1995). Although successive generations of faculty at research universities publish more than those not at these institutions, it is likely that it is as much a matter of personal choice, fulfillment, and field advancement as it is institutional expectation for merit, tenure, and promotion. The expectation is survival. Survival implies a competitive spirit that may overlook civility in favor of success. This competitive environment invites bullying. For instance, a bully approaches an untenured faculty member and offers coauthorship opportunities or even a coeditorship. The naive new faculty member embraces the chance to publish with a renowned author and assumes the offers are legitimate. He or she needs tenure or help publishing in order to compete in higher education. The bully gets more entries on his or her curriculum vitae and boasts of mentoring young colleagues. In reality, this person is holding the unsuspecting faculty member hostage for some later purpose, such as aligning with him or her on a pivotal committee vote or supporting the person for department chair, dean, or promotion to full professor.

What do faculty need to succeed in an environment stressing competition, dominance, and power? Salin (2003) argued they need a supportive, motivating organizational structure and a cooperative, enabling academic culture. This culture is as likely to enable mentoring as it is incivility and bullying.

4

Motivating Structures and Processes
Academic Organization and Governance Structure

*Academe, with its rigid hierarchy in what is supposed
to be a collaborative culture, is a natural incubator for
conflict.*

Piper Fogg

Universities are hives of intrigue and conspiracy.

David Kember

Organizational structures in higher education institutions look
like a bureaucracy yet function through shared governance.
These motivating structures coupled with imbalances of power may
interact to facilitate maladaptive environments that may invite
and sustain incivility. The university is one of a few organizations
where the faculty *is* the university, yet the faculty is employed *by*
the university. In other words, the administration is both master of
and servant to the faculty (Adams, 1988).

Because universities are large and complex, they house multiple
power and governance centers. The university is a hierarchical
business organization and an academic institution simultaneously.
Traditionally universities have emphasized and practiced shared
governance. More recently, however, power has shifted to management and administration (Bergquist, 1992; Lewis, 2004; White,
2004). Within the hierarchy, faculty self-govern to a greater or
lesser extent (Kerr, 1982); some institutions function with more

centralization while others are more decentralized (Minor, 2004). Self-governance within a bureaucratic hierarchy causes varying levels of conflict among faculty and between faculty and administration. While the university governance structure may be designed to resolve conflict, it also has the potential to shield, protect, and encourage it. The desire for more money in the university budget lubricates the system and keeps it progressing, but perhaps moving too fast for the administration to address resurfacing conflicts that arise as a result of issues directly and indirectly related to scarce financial resources. Or perhaps the money motive camouflages or whitewashes the conflicts.

Blau (1994) posited that how an organization is configured affects the academic work inside. In other words, the larger the university is, the greater the likelihood there is of centralization. Centralization typically diminishes autonomy, particularly of academic specialists like faculty, who self-govern and evaluate themselves. Historically, as a university grew larger and became more centralized, it was unable to address resource allocation to mesh with the myriad changes. Decentralization, which followed, attempted to preserve autonomy but instead created more and deeper isolation of campus units. Horizontal decision making occurred in each separate unit, but little or no contact between units occurred (Benjamin & Carroll, 1998). Autonomy and decentralization produced more cosmopolitan perspectives on academic specialties, while centralization produced more orientation to the institution (Gouldner, 1957, 1958; Merton, 1949). Faculties became less a community of scholars and more a community of incivility.

Berger and Luckman (1967) acknowledged that institutions in theory "hang together"; that is, each component part contributes something to the collective whole. Academics coexist based on their respective roles, interests, and abilities, all of which are important to the institution's social structure. Individual faculty members choose to focus on instruction, while others focus on their research. Researchers may focus on writing articles, books, or textbooks. Still other faculty focus on service, such as running for faculty senate, accepting the position of journal editor, or being a conference program director. Faculty members are happy to make a contribution and carve out a niche, but as they do, they compete for scarce resources or key power positions; eventually, the realities of these rather individually constructed worlds conflict and collide. Gouldner (1957, 1958) explained that loyalty to the institution by some faculty is pitted against loyalty to the discipline by others.

One of the main bargaining chips faculty retain in a centralized bureaucracy is selecting colleagues. Selecting one candidate over another could determine the direction a department will take in the future (Lang, 2005). Most faculty searches are a national effort rather than a local effort, known as inbreeding. Blau (1994) saw inbreeding as paternalistic and favoring administration goals and agendas, not faculty disciplinary growth. Actions such as these open the door for conflict between faculty and administration and among colleagues. Hiring someone whose presence will change the department direction allows for repercussion, especially if one group of faculty in a department is wedded to one candidate, and another group supports the contender (Lang, 2005). These battles can be heated.

I talked to one faculty colleague with whom I had a collegial relationship, and he said, "This is just the way we handle it at the school district level." But as time went on, he too realized there was something wrong, as nothing was ever getting accomplished. For instance, if we had a choice to make and A was chosen, those who wanted B went off and did what they wanted. — Caroline

Faculty meetings became much more intense — nothing gets done . . . and we go nowhere. — Ben

---

To a greater or lesser degree, power is wielded by both faculty, as the self-governed, and administrators, as appointed bureaucrats in a power relations duel. The struggle for this power and perceived entitlement may give rise to increased workplace incivility and harassment opportunities (McCarthy, 2003). Power shifts and struggles may manifest themselves in behaviors that fall outside the parameters of civility. Incivility may be allowed to persist as an informal mode of social control used to indoctrinate new members and, ultimately, ensure long-term group affiliation and identity. Uncivil behavior may also result as faculty struggle to maintain traditional values in the face of the administration's push for change. Uncivil behavior may be the residual from increased competition and conflict.

Part of the social construction of incivility may be legitimized as a means for some entrants and incumbents to gain parity in the organization (McCarthy, 2003). It could also mean parity within a new position, as when faculty move into administrative roles. It may be reflective of society in general and the biosocial nature of humanity in particular, working in tandem with these organizational factors. This chapter examines whether normative standards constitute acceptable behavior in an organization and if the organization tolerates incivility and bullying.

Shared Governance and Faculty Self-Governance

Faculty self-governance, common to the collegium, came from French, German, and British universities (Altbach & Finkestein, 1997). Lynton (1995) advocated that to ensure a properly functioning institution, faculty must be good "institutional citizens." In reality, committees, the hallmark of shared governance, are slow to resolve most issues (Dziech & Weiner, 1990) indicating that perhaps all faculty members are not always good citizens all the time.

Julius, Baldridge, and Pfeffer (1999) noted that what they call "people-processing" institutions like colleges and universities have many, though often ambiguous, goals. The pursuit of those goals could permit one individual to motivate others to move in a calculated direction through the faculty committee structure. Furthermore, committees theoretically consist of experts who make decisions on major issues. However, university committee work is not necessarily a faculty member's primary concern or area of expertise; a faculty member's major concern is his or her own discipline and scholarship. Committee power usually vests itself in those who have an interest in the committee decision outcome.

. One male faculty had been a member on the merit pay committee —not the chair but [he] used his power as leverage. When he talked, people would tend not to cross him. There was a woman on the committee, but the women were quiet in the department and just accepted the treatment they were handed. That's the culture here. — Caroline

---

While specific issues, new faculty, goals, and decisions come and go and come again, the faculty stalwarts remain to see it all and perhaps wield accrued power. It may be that shared governance is theoretically desirable, but the reality can be less than desirable. We illustrate with promotion and tenure.

Incivility and the Tenure and Promotion Process

Tenure and promotion processes are often shrouded in secrecy and mystery, and promotion and tenure documents are often open to multiple interpretation. Sorcinelli (2002) described them as frequently "ambiguous, shifting, and inconsistent," more stringent as time passes, and often devoid of helpful feedback (p. 42). As a result, new faculty rarely seek clarification for fear of showing weaknesses and vulnerabilities.

Wright (2005), who explored promotion and tenure documents at research institutions, noted that they offer lip-service to the importance of teaching but in reality often favor and reward research pursuits, in the process sending ambiguous messages. Communication ambiguity occurs when faculty receive poorly defined messages or inconsistent feedback.

In addition to misunderstanding the document on the part of new faculty, promotion and tenure committee members are tasked with making comparisons across time and across dossiers, which is even more tenuous, and rather like comparing apples to oranges (Blau, 1994). What was expected of senior colleagues twenty years ago may not be the standard expected now. Are eight articles in top-tier journals equal to sixteen articles in lesser-known journals? Faculty can identify bad teaching more clearly than good teaching. Perhaps one reason for this is that faculty members are more highly suited to judge peers on research-related matters because that is where their competence lies. Their discipline or profession provides them with a standard against which to evaluate peer research contributions. However, evaluation of teaching is more individual and more nebulous because faculty, being less competent in pedagogy, have difficulty evaluating teaching by the same rigid standard that research is evaluated. As a result, they undergo peer review, but that review may be done by someone not competent in pedagogy.

In highly specialized organizations like academe that demand a deep level of commitment and engagement, the structure of the organization can render employees vulnerable (Abdennur, 2000; Coyne, Craig, & Smith-Lee Chong, 2004; Ferris, 2004; Gayle, Bhoendradatt, & White, 2003; Smith, Singer, Hoel, & Cooper, 2003). Abdennur (2000) noted that uncivil behaviors often go undetected because they may be embedded within what appears to be a functioning organization structure. For instance, each member of a promotion and tenure committee has a slightly different interpretation of what constitutes "good" teaching, "effective" service, or "outstanding" scholarship as set out in the tenure and promotion document (Twale & Lane, 2006). Most likely those interpretations stem from how and where the members were socialized and where and how they themselves first received tenure. The potential for disparity between members' interpretations and vantage points creates dissonance. As Berger and Luckman (1967) said, "There is an ongoing correspondence between *my* messages and *their* meanings" (p. 23). In fact, we do not all interpret information in exactly the same way. Interpretations are not problematic, however, if they can be absorbed, integrated, or managed.

Problems and situations that cannot be dealt with in the confines of the existing reality can result in "enclaves" (Berger & Luckman, 1967, p. 25), which are signified when new meanings and realities are attached to them. Because academic governance functions through committees and correct interpretations can be as likely as misinterpretations, these processes can conceal aggressive individual faculty member behaviors through groupthink mentality and groupthink practices (Janis, 1982, 1988). What may appear on the surface to be a functional committee may house an enclave that operates differently than would be thought normative. Abdennur (2000) contended that uncivil behavior may be present as a result of those misinterpretations, but if it is camouflaged within the self-governance structure, it can appear normative.

I recall serving on the P&T committee a few years ago when we had a huge representation of women on the committee. When a male faculty member didn't receive tenure, the committee changed the following year to be overwhelmingly male. How the change occurred was subverted. Other members and I were dismissed and subsequently slandered. Others not on the committee, as well as some remaining on the committee, were complicit in the "overthrow." — Abby

---

Berger and Luckman (1967) discussed the reality of personal interaction and regarded intersubjective encounters as flexible, such that it is "difficult to impose rigid patterns upon face-to-face interaction" (p. 30). Given the typical academic self-governance, business is conducted by committees charged with making recommendations to administrators. In promotion and tenure proceedings especially, it is possible, based on Berger and Luckman's premise, for members to misinterpret matters based on their own interpretation of the policy document or the materials contained in the candidate dossiers or the oral and written assessments of senior evaluators. Like Milgram's experiments (1963), tenure and promotion committee processes remove the interaction from face-to-face interactions where actions are more likely to be fully observed. Confidential proceedings often mask the real interpretation or misinterpretation of committee members toward candidates.

Confidentiality also hides real action from full view or scrutiny. As Baez (2002) warned, "Confidentiality may protect the integrity of peer review, but it also hinders things" (p. 170). Rarely questioned, confidentiality is standard practice in academic hiring, firing, tenure, promotion, evaluations, and peer review. What might be standard to safeguard the integrity of the peer review process may also be an acceptable means to sanitize or cover the truth. While confidentiality is regarded as necessary, the veil of secrecy is damning for individuals if it involves politics and power plays that cover bias, discrimination, hate, or other destructive acts (Giebel, 2005; Klein, 2005).

Under the guise of academic freedom and autonomy, faculty committees could camouflage uncivil behaviors and underlying motives such that one or more faculty member's maneuverings could emerge as sanitized and acceptable in collectively reported and confidentially sealed committee decisions (Abdennur, 2000; Lewis, 2004). For instance, the promotion and tenure document and committee deliberation is perhaps the most powerful in academe because it validates faculty careers. Tenured and promoted faculty members appointed or elected to that committee control the future rank and status of candidates (Bollinger, 2005; Rayner, Hoel, & Cooper, 2002). It is the perfect setting for bullying to take place. On a promotion and tenure committee, the bully can interpret credentials in the way he or she feels will benefit him or her the most, regardless of what is best for the candidate, department, or institution. The bully can also deny any involvement in an unpopular decision by hiding behind the groupthink deliberation or claiming to have "voted differently," knowing that those not on the committee will never know the actual vote or the nature of the deliberations.

Chronicling her story of tenure denial, Abramson (1975) alluded to the secrecy among administrators, the committee filtering the decisions, the lack of consistency to which rules and policies were followed, and the downplaying of conflicting challenges. Abramson analogized her plight to that of a leper, with colleagues going out of their way to avoid her. Disengagement, duty reduction, and invisibility followed. Female colleagues whom she thought would be supportive seemed suspicious or resentful of her actions. As Glazer-Raymo (1999) reminded us, we camouflage tenure denial in the closed meeting of the promotion and tenure committee deliberations.

Pamela Haag (2005), a sex discrimination expert, saw the way academe treats tenure decision cases involving women as often flying under existing policy radar. In other words, the acts are subtle and therefore difficult to prosecute effectively and with redress. Victims may feel used or uncomfortable, but those feelings of discomfort are not clearly articulated in existing policy. Haag described academe in loose terms because faculty and administrators create documents formulated with "subjective" and "nebulous" criteria and "broad definitions of scholarship," such as those used in tenure policies. Under these circumstances and given these broad terms and parameters, it is challenging to match such arbitrary standards with the reality that is needed in court proceedings. As such, faculty make exceptions for some situations but not others and may change over time and with circumstance, and that affects how faculty have viewed their governance role in academe. It affects how each views each other too.

I admit that I had no trouble getting tenure, but my pretenure review was bizarre. The summary comments for teaching, research, and service were very accurate, supportive, and complimentary. The section on collegiality, however, stated that because I was quiet, no one really knew me. I didn't think it was congeniality, but that was what I was being measured on, not collegiality. Either they did not know what the term meant, or my quiet persona was threatening to them because they didn't know what I was doing. I ran the letter by a lawyer who laughed and said, "You have tenure now." He suggested I write a response to the department chair asking how the tenured faculty and I might get to know one another. I never heard from anyone. — Abby

---

Unfortunately, what has meaning has relevance (Berger & Luckman, 1967). Committee members give meaning to the policy document as well as to the candidate dossiers. Their collective decision has paramount relevance to the future of the candidate. Junior faculty fate is vested in the power of the committee, and these committee proceedings can be contentious, heated, tense, and gut wrenching. Depending on who constitutes the committee across time, who influences, and who guides the power plays determines if decisions meet normative standards of the past or deviate from them (Keashly & Jagatic, 2003; Van Alstyne, 1997).

Chism's study (2006) found that teaching awards provided a perfect example of how vague directives are written and distributed to a faculty committee trying ethically and fairly to bestow special awards on peers. In the absence of clear performance criteria, guidelines, standards, and evidence, the awards render little real or symbolic value. She pointed out that the outcomes absent of solid guidelines will be shrouded in "mystery, distrust, and unexamined personal beliefs of the judges . . . [becoming] . . . simply popularity contests" (p. 609). The chances for unfair treatment of colleagues and peers increase under these circumstances. When committees fail to follow guidelines for any reason and are challenged by neither colleagues nor the administrator, the award, the process, the committee members, and the administrator lose credibility. The process becomes uncivil.

I have always been suspicious of a particular incident in which the victim of an initial tenure denial (later overturned) used an award committee appointment to refuse an award to a person on that initial tenure committee when the individual would likely have received the award at institutions more prestigious than this one. It is really odd because the tenure candidate seemed to know or thought he knew how the confidential deliberations went. I actually did bring the issue to the attention of the administrators, both verbally and in writing. I was assured that the procedures would be changed for the future. The bully just found another way around the procedures the following year. The bully remains on the committee. — Kathy

---

Support from the Governance Structure

One would expect that because faculty often work in isolated environments, the chance of interpersonal aggressiveness falls. However, aggressiveness may take alternative forms due to the academic governance structure. Faculty members who are introverted may be waiting victims. If the institutional structure inadvertently normalizes or sanitizes bullying, it may come to have value for some faculty and thus be practiced more readily (Salin, 2003).

The faculty member also begins to believe that no repercussions, or at least no severe ones for uncivil or bullying behavior, are anticipated. Faculty see that the bounds are limitless to where power and authority extend or where it is unconstrained, and more important, probably no one will notice it anyway. This freedom is provocative, intoxicating, and contagious. It can create self-aggrandizement and entice some faculty to proclaim godlike status for themselves (Dziech & Weiner, 1990). This status becomes an invitation to be uncivil to others in the workplace.

Damrosch (1995) depicted the university as an antibureaucracy: "the greatest possible number of individuals . . . pursue their own private interests with the least possible interaction" (p. 59) with colleagues. Because faculty seldom seem to be held accountable, department faculty can dominate and control the rest of the department and subtly and passively recruit and secure new members to maintain that critical hold on the status quo. This critical hold could be demographic or philosophical. Because faculty more often work in isolation than collaboration, faculty members may fail "to cultivate working relationships"; therefore, department business is conducted through "a mixture of private patronage and part time power-brokering" (p. 75).

I felt I was discriminated against without civility in my department in a more underhanded way when I was asked to serve on a committee. I was absolutely too busy to do it because I felt so overwhelmed. My declining that request caused a cascade of other things to happen. At some point, I was given an overload above accreditation norms while colleagues had half my load. The refusals continued. When I wrote for an internal grant, I was refused. However, a comment made it to the dean's office. When the dean found out we had none of the materials

I was seeking through the grant, the dean went to my department chair and asked why. Things changed after that. — Lucille

---

Bureaucracy, Isolation, and Incivility

The sheer size of institutional faculties housed by disciplinary specializations and subspecializations increases the likelihood of academic silos. Size also dictates the level of bureaucracy needed to run the institution and the number of committees needed for self-governance (Altbach & Finkelstein, 1997). Academe consists also of levels of faculty rank and status that ultimately determine faculty power and prestige. In a bureaucratic structure like the university, where power is disbursed throughout a large organization, Sennett (1976) claimed two things usually happen: (1) responsibility for any one act by any one person is assumed and (2) protection from full accountability as a result of the largesse usually occurs. He said amnesia often follows in the latter case as people forget what they do to others. Bennis (1989) concurred: "Bureaucracies are beautiful mechanisms for the evasion of responsibility and guilt" (p. 96), and thus are breeding grounds for uncivil action.

Obviously I am deeply hurt by the treatment I see this person make toward others, including the group of "yes-men" she has gathered around her and who also treat some others in bully fashion. More troubling to me is that the current dean is a person who, when I was dean, I hired . . . , promoted, mentored, and gave the opportunity to publish. . . . Now that she is dean, there is absolutely no recognition of the opportunities and support I provided her. Essentially the unspoken feeling directed toward me is, "It's now my show; you are no longer wanted and will be marginalized." — Doug

---

Because shared governance processes move relatively slowly, changing traditional values and ideals may gain momentum but move slowly over time. Much like the lobster does not know it is about to become the main course, some faculty choose to ignore the gradually warming waters of the administrative changes. Also given that the university is loosely coupled (Weick, 1976), changes are easier to implement in the bureaucracy but not as easily accepted culturally or within a tightly held faculty self-governance structure (Schuster and associates, 1994). The 370 years of values and tradition in higher education are difficult to change quickly or radically. Change increases incongruence and lowers morale among faculty and trust toward administration. It also overburdens the system and increases divisiveness, frustration, confusion, chaos, dysfunction, and disruption. In her case study of an institution facing changes in governance, Kezar (2005) noticed that certain academic factions were being marginalized. She chronicled the presence of demoralization, cynicism, and poor participation that hampered the development of a new governance model to replace the old one, which relied heavily on self-governance. The result became a difficult pill to swallow.

Bennis (1989) wrote that each new member of the university hierarchy arrives with basic human "sensitivities, fragilities, and needs" (p. 77). Instability following change opens a door for stronger faculty personalities to take advantage of weaker colleagues. The governance structure allows them to use their power in an uncivil way, especially if their goal is self-preservation in the face of change. As a result, White (2004) suggested, organizational structures and these concomitant imbalances of power interact to facilitate maladaptive environments. Incivility may result from the power imbalance inherent in the organizational self-governance structure in terms of how it is wielded through either human or symbolic means (Hoel, Faragher, & Cooper, 2004; Hoel & Salin, 2003; Rayner, Hoel, & Cooper, 2002). Incivility and bullying or mobbing may be another means that stronger, more powerful faculty and administrators use to ensure conformity to new or modified organizational goals even though they contrast with traditional norms and values (Ironside & Seifert, 2003). Because this is commonplace during times of change, faculty may not be aware they are bullying colleagues or subordinates to ensure conformity.

I have also seen bullying fail. In department efforts to make some program adjustment, a bully tried to exert undue pressure on a less dominant personality, only to find out that in fact the less dominant personality was not "less" at all. This put the bully in a very unfamiliar situation, but it did not cause the perpetrator to back off but rather only back up to regroup and try another tactic. — Kathy

---

Movement toward new norms may unintentionally sanction incivility as a means of social control. Unfortunately for faculty, hazing-like behavior comes to be accepted over time as customary (Ferris, 2004; Gayle, Bhoendradatt, & White, 2003; Hadikin & O'Driscoll, 2000; Rayner, Hoel, & Cooper, 2002). New faculty who speak out at faculty meetings before they understand the prevailing culture are often reprimanded by being shunned, belittled, or dismissed until they learn protocol and that respect is owed more senior colleagues. Many academics experienced similar treatment as graduate students, so they assume that it must be part of the career journey. Some students are asked to write and rewrite their dissertation many times and wait months for feedback from professors. Tenure and promotion committee procedures are often touted as hazing rituals as well. As a result, faculty do not question such behavior, they are too intimidated or fearful to report it, or there is no structured avenue through which to address it in the hierarchy or through trusted self-governance means.

I was surprised to experience hazing as a graduate student, not once, but continually and by multiple professors. I mentioned to another graduate assistant that I wanted to make a formal complaint, but he discouraged me from doing that. I watched how some of the other women faculty members in the department were treated, and they were second-class citizens at best. So I came to realize that that is the way it was in *that* discipline at *that* institution. If I didn't like it, I needed to transfer to another discipline or another institution, and they would surely be nicer to me. The place I transferred to was better. — Abby

Gender Issues

Bureaucracies have traditionally been led by men; therefore, gender has been introduced as a means to determine power and status within the organization. In other words, bureaucracy has been more likely to serve the interests of majority males than any other group, regardless of the situation. The university is no different. Aquirre (2000) offered a continuum of difference as a reference point used by the majority group to determine if gender differences threaten the status quo or, at the other extreme, modify the existing bureaucratic structure to be more inclusive and accepting. In the final analysis, it all depends on whether the values, habits, attitudes, and beliefs of the newcomers are valued by the gatekeepers. Despite their visibility, women and minority groups may appear invisible because the organizational hierarchy has been encouraged to recruit members of these specific groups whose credentials may or may not align with current departmental standards. But the goal may be one of visibility as opposed to building a strong department. Specifically, the bureaucracy has scaffolding capabilities and loose coupling to procure the wants of a different group with different career goals and expectations (Weick, 1976). The rewards and socialization designed by white men for white men, however, are often slow to accommodate nonwhite male groups (Aquirre, 2000). For instance, Nidiffer (2001) noted that "structural barriers [and organizational culture] can thwart women presidents with overt criticism, harassment, or more subtle forms of discomfort." Furthermore, women at any level also can experience "exclusion, hostility, and neglect" (p. 121).

Meetings were male dominated. A tenured full female prof gets up to talk, and an untenured junior faculty man tells her that her ideas are not really important, that it may be a concern of hers but not ours. And the entire faculty went along with it, *including* the women. He said what she put forward was useless. . . . Gender on gender was very strong. Be invisible. We weren't supposed to say anything, even the strong women who could hold their own. Women sensed they were in a powerless position. — Caroline

---

Based on a study of harassment grievances that academic women filed between 1970 and 1983, one common response from women who filed grievances was their "fear of antagonizing male colleagues" (Farley, 1985, p. 112) and reinforcing their own vulnerability in the workplace. At the time of the study, few women had entered the academic ranks, the normative standards favored white males, harassment policies were fewer in number, and little precedence favoring women had been set. Thus, under the prevailing circumstances, women showed reluctance to challenge the system in anticipation of repercussions perhaps much worse than the original harassment. Dziech and Weiner (1990) continued the discussion on sexual harassment as it began to affect gender relationships in academe in their provocative book, *The Lecherous Professor*. One key concern Farley mentioned with regard to the university governance process was the assumption of committee confidentiality, which portends an implied power inherent in faculty self-governance that at the time of the study was mostly male.

In fact, women are less likely to participate in governance or committee activities, especially the more critical committees like promotion and tenure (Twale & Shannon, 1996). Women are more likely to express displeasure with the committee structure if committee assignments are viewed as gendered placements. Women may be tokens. It may appear to male colleagues that women are being given power and status, but that may not be the case (Aquirre, 2000).

Job insecurity associated with untenured status or unrealistic performance expectations can also be a recipe for faculty victimization (McCarthy & Mayhew, 2004). Placing minority and women junior faculty members on multiple collegewide and universitywide committees to fulfill service requirements borders on incivility if they become overtaxed tokens. In other words, organizations can legitimize camouflaged aggression within their formal bureaucratic structure. This camouflaged incivility not only harbors deception but also enables the perpetrators who assign these tasks to insulate themselves from taking any responsibility for their behavior because committee service is part of the university mission *and* a faculty obligation. The token is the only one who suffers.

Bureaupathology

According to Bennis (1989), universities are "underled and over-managed" (p. 18). The unempowered feel insignificant and often find themselves cocooning, siloing, and isolating themselves from their colleagues. Eventually academic work produces a cadre of ego-centered professionals. This phenomenon has two sides: one side produces isolated academics who quietly take their work seriously and the other ego-centered academics who take both their work and themselves seriously. The latter may be uncivil to the former, and the former could allow themselves to be ill treated by the latter in an unhealthy bureaucracy.

[My take on bullying is that it] is using words that demean another person intellectually or suggest that the person is misguided and just doesn't understand. This is often done in public to add additional insult and humiliation to the recipient of the bullying behavior. Incivility persists for many reasons, but perhaps the largest issue is unfettered ego at work. If I can get away with treating others this way, then I *can* get away with it. — Doug

---

If we merge micromanagement common to ineffective admin-istrators in some universities with the fact that the university faculty members are ego centered, we have a situation ripe for what Abdennur (2000) labeled *bureaupathology*. With a lack of leadership and an overabundance of big egos and middle managers, incivility and aggression can be easily masked in the system. It is entirely pos-sible that in the absence of good leadership, victimized academics cocoon themselves in order to render their lives more livable. With the university administration leaning more to a bureaucratic and corporate focus, they may have created a silent upheaval among academics, who have adopted one of two responses: open fighting or retreating to their work. Bennis (1989) insisted that administra-tors manage the money rather than lead the organization, causing faculty to go their own way and work in ways that are egocentrically driven. Incivility likely increases under these circumstances.

My colleagues will occasionally tell me that they are dissatisfied with the administration, so they found other interests. I found that I don't come to the office as often as I used to. I justify being home as a way to complete work. I have thrown myself into my work, making more of it so I can further justify not going into work daily. I discovered through consulting that other people value me and my work, so I too have found other avenues to be successful and to retreat from my own institution and my colleagues with whom I have little in common anymore. It has made me feel better about myself, but I still recognize the detriment to isolating myself from them. — Abby

---

This is not to say that these professionals operate totally with intentional malice toward the organization or their colleagues. Egos in higher education can be likened to molecules in a microwave: the more they bump into one another, the more heat they generate. The more isolated the egos are, the less likely they are to collide with fellow egos. However, the contentious issues remain whether egos seek silos. For instance, a collegial debate among equals who have equal voice in the matter may produce an energizing and invigorating dialogue. A debate between faculty and administration, where the power is unequal, the stakes are high, and the resources finite, could have fewer civil results and consequences.

I had a former dean who for lack of a better descriptor was one mean SOB. When I did something that other colleagues and I thought would be beneficial to the growth of the program I coordinated, he took great offense. Instead of having a civilized conversation about it, he summoned me to his office, closed the door, yelled at me, shook his finger in my face, and insinuated what a bad girl I had been. His anger scared me, and it was terribly offensive to a senior colleague. — Abby

---

Faculty dissatisfaction with administration could signal the presence of incivility (Hoel & Salin, 2003). Kezar (2005) also found that where one sits in the organization affects one's perspective on leadership and administration and how it functions (or malfunctions). Faculty who see themselves as empowered lead and act quite differently from faculty who view their relative positioning as servants to the administration or as simple paper pushers.

Although faculty and administration work in the same general environment, each group views its environment differently based on its unique vantage point. A faculty member resocialized into a new role as administrator often directs his or her efforts toward the institution and seemingly away from former colleagues. Change initiated by administration is often slowed by faculty. Top-down power wielding inadvertently destroys collegiality and, according to Benjamin and Carroll (1998), causes more harm than good. If faculty and administrative goals conflict, then incongruence in the workplace can lead to tension, low morale, competition, and low career satisfaction (Blackburn & Lawrence, 1995). According to Keashly and Jagatic (2003), the norms of the workplace appear likely to precipitate uncivil action.

In business and industry where there are superordinate and subordinate dyads, superordinates can legitimately control the behavior of subordinates (French & Raven, 1960). Academe functions similarly in that the university is a bureaucracy, but the academic side functions differently from the bureaucracy because professionals have privilege. Faculty rank has privilege apart from administrative line positions. While line positions hold authority, persons in nonadministrative faculty positions may amass greater power across campus over time. Power may arise out of scholarly accomplishment, impressive grantsmanship, or outstanding service on key university committees. Professional capital banked and invested over time renders some faculty more influential than some seated administrators (Keashly & Jagatic, 2003).

Every fall we have a collegewide meeting. It is a time for the dean to acknowledge personal accomplishments and offer a self-developed strategic plan for the new academic year. One year he told the whole faculty that he mentioned to a colleague at another institution that he had just hired [person's name] to our faculty. The colleague's response was, "His presence will lift your faculty up." Our dean took that as a supreme compliment. I know I wasn't the only person incensed and demeaned by that comment. Each one of the faculty in our college makes a contribution, but it seemed that the new kid on the block would be destined to be the dean's most prized accomplishment. — Abby

---

Rosenzweig's study (1998) of twelve former university presidents showed that they act in ways that harbor resentment and suspicion of fellow faculty. Even as top administrators, they fear the power of the faculty, who can cause them to topple from their jobs. Rosenzweig noted that "faculty are the most powerful single force in the university . . . because they either . . . carry the institution forward . . . or . . . stop it in its tracks" (p. 158).

The increased call for accountability has eroded some faculty professional power, which will likely adversely affect the professoriat. This perceived loss of power often leads to political maneuvering. Fashioning themselves as autonomous, independent scholars, faculty members often clash with the administration's desire for accountability. Furthermore, financial constraints have caused university administrators to infringe on traditional faculty autonomy (Altbach & Finkelstein, 1997).

Politics, Power, and Incivility

Julius, Baldridge, and Pfeffer (1999) have portrayed the academic institution as one that is "challenged and highly political" and "reflects competing groups who often conflict" (p. 116). In addition, "Anyone who seeks to transcend the status quo will be met with opposition" (p. 116), and that is why peers serve as gatekeepers. For example, the professional expectation of peer review implies the quality control of experts over one's disciplinary colleagues. Peer reviewers of manuscripts act as gatekeepers for their respective professions. They hold the power to print or squash an idea, technique, discovery, or research paradigm. Scrutiny may be editorial and grammatical, but it may also be equally political and uncivil (Berkenkotter, 1995).

Adams (1988) began his discussion of academic politics with the notion that power in the academy is diffused because it exists in diffused pockets across the institution. But sometimes it only seems that way. For instance, Adams noted, a faculty candidate who does not receive tenure is likely to be a pariah in the department in the lame duck period between tenure committee decision and buffer year. Passive-avoidance behaviors by colleagues, no matter how well intended, are still passive forms of incivility that could be categorized as estrangement.

The Matthew effect exemplifies the principle of cumulative advantage, where those who have are more likely than those who do not have to secure more. Jobs in academe have varying resources and opportunities depending on where they are located and how they are classified. Faculty in intellectually rich, highly supportive environments are more likely to prosper, succeed, and advance than faculty relegated to meager environments. In other words, prestige begets prestige, and mediocrity begets prestige only rarely. For example, placement in the first academic position affects career productivity and perhaps placement in subsequent career positions (McGinnis & Long, 1998). The need to overcome perceived or real disadvantage implies the presence of a political mechanism through which one may rise above the mediocrity or strive to hold on to prestige. However, some faculty use the political route to overcome what they call "distributive injustice," that is, to right what they perceive as unjust in their meager circumstances. This dissatisfaction and frustration with the organization based on perceived or real unfair practices and processes could lead a person to justify uncivil acts (Neuman & Baron, 2003).

Organizational survival-of-the-fittest norms often encourage micropolitics through the use of uncivil, bully, or mob behaviors (Neuman & Baron, 2003). In these instances, discussion turns to argumentation, posturing, and contention. Senior faculty members with power jockey into position. Those with power or perceived power and some authority may see their position power as forcing a win-lose outcome (Bennis, 1989). As a result, some senior faculty members may aggressively or passive-aggressively pressure dissenters into supporting them in order to protect their territory or position. This political maneuvering could be construed as camouflaged aggression, and the weak may feel obliged to comply.

Douglass (1986) wrote, "Institutions create shadowed places in which nothing can be seen and no questions asked" (p. 69). These areas are not considered or even known to exist because other areas that are visible are highly visible. We see those visible areas and think we have seen enough or all that is needed to be seen. But it is the shadowy places that may need the closest scrutiny. Nevertheless, we are satisfied by what we see outside the shadows, and if enough of it is good or at least livable, we do not pursue what we cannot see. As a result, the warning signs of conflict and incivility may be overlooked or ignored in the bureaucracy and the self-governance structure. The culture of the organization harbors many purposefully hidden places, as we show in Chapter Five. Here we inadvertently implant the seeds that allow incivility to expand in an enabling structure.

5

Enabling Structure and Process
The Academic Culture

*Cultures are provocative and full of dangerous
ambiguities.*

Eric Gould

The unique organizational structure of the university supports
an equally unique academic culture. As in any other group,
cultural artifacts, trends, norms, folkways, mores, and taboos are
present everywhere, yet no two academic cultures are exactly the
same. Cultures change over time as new colleagues enter and older
faculty members retire, are promoted to administrative positions,
or seek jobs elsewhere. In this chapter, we first examine culture as
an anthropological concept and then look at academic culture in
terms of how incivility can be harbored within it. The academic
culture is a breeding ground for incivility, bullying, and mobbing.

Culture Defined

Culture, defined as the values, ideologies, and beliefs that determine
a group's way of life, embodies perceptions held by those in the group
who interpret those values and beliefs (Eagleton, 2000). Culture
is a combination of the sacred, the profane, the ceremonious, and
the routine. In a sense, it is a secular religion.

Culture supports the need to preserve. We think of culture as
lasting forever, but actually it is fragile and vulnerable. In fact, a

culture harbors self-preservation and survival mechanisms because the dormant seeds of the culture's own destruction are found within it. Although culture is presumed to be unifying, it also supports subgroups or subcultures and, often, a counterculture. Bully cultures are the essence of that counterculture. Culture tolerates stress, conflict, and confusion in bearable amounts. In general, it recognizes actions as normative or disruptive. Fortunately, however, culture is regenerative, reflective, and evolving. It seeks to survive through whatever means exist when its values are threatened, including bullying others to see things their way.

Culture is not culture until it is shared. Culture has an image of itself, shared by its supporters, that is grounded in history, interpreted in folklore, and shrouded in mystique (Eagleton, 2000). Accounts of that culture may vary depending on the storyteller and his or her unique vantage point and the interpretation of the account. One member of the culture may view his or her department as a wonderful place to work, and another may dread going to work every day.

As a beacon, culture towers over us, lights our way, and beckons us home (Eagleton, 2000). At the same time, it expects us, its members, to relinquish a part of ourselves to fully adhere to its formal and informal standards and norms. Bullies ask their victims to do the same, but the loyalty is to them or the bully culture rather than the institution. Because culture embodies the conscious and the unconscious, observers can only attest to what they see other members doing or what has been documented; the rest cannot be known or presumed because it is the part shrouded in mystery. Bullying through committee deliberations tends to remain shrouded in mystery.

To protect and preserve the culture against internal and external threats requires the members to seek harmony (Eagleton, 2000). Harmony may require political action. Culture requires allegiance from members whose actions to preserve it may be devoid of rationality but may promote harmony. Culture encourages change, as Eagleton characterizes, but often the changes are hauntingly as recognizable as before (see also Lévi-Strauss, 1963). We alter ourselves while being altered by forces in the culture; usually these forces are political in nature. Therefore, to master the politics is to master the culture (Eagleton, 2000). To master the bully or the mob is to master the situation.

Culture tolerates mild abuses and disengagements but seldom tolerates or survives mass overthrows, major upheavals, or gross transitions (Eagleton, 2000). Culture is constructive when threatened from the outside and destructive when faced with internal threat. Culture circles the wagons to resist harm from the outside but challenges itself and its internal actions in a less organized fashion. Some of the most loyal members of culture can be destructive to it. Some of these loyal members may be the bullies or the mob. While culture is normative and seeks homeostasis, it harbors and must deal with these extreme behavioral types (Eagleton, 2000; Williams, 1976). Some of these types exhibit conflict, confrontation, temper tantrums, and other bully behaviors (Ruger & Bickel, 2004).

Culture portends freedom of expression, but also readily and often harshly critiques it. Members may oppose the very nature of their culture yet decline to criticize it (Eagleton, 2000; von Herder, 2000; Young, 1995). To criticize the culture would be to criticize ourselves because we are in the culture, and culture is in us. Without the critique, however, the culture is less likely to evolve or identify the bully.

When I worked in a large department, it became apparent to the newcomers how dysfunctional it really was. To the faculty who had been there for decades, it was normal. They thought nothing of sweet-talking new faculty into helping them with projects or getting some of us to put their names on the research we were doing.

They did it with graduate assistants too. As much as I and some of my other colleagues wanted to tell them how dysfunctional the department was and how unethical it was, we were afraid to do so, so we just gravitated away from them. — Abby

---

Entrants into the culture must be accepted by the current members and socialized to accept and support the prevailing values and ideologies and know the laws and policies that govern the culture. Faculty are as likely to accept the bad with the good, but not to speak out against a bully culture is submissive acceptance of it.

Knowledge and acceptance are prerequisites to claiming any power and authority over other members of the culture (Eagleton, 2000; Said, 1993). Without recognition of the power it takes to eradicate a bully culture, it will prevail. Culture is insular and molds its members so much that when they are steeped too heavily in it, the culture blinds them to all other things. Culture may be so engrained by the majority of members as to go unnoticed by them, but it will surely be reflected in the actions of new entrants and subversives who have not fully embraced the culture (Bourdieu, 1977).

I will never forget a September departmental faculty meeting when we welcomed five new faculty members. During the meeting, an old guard faculty member explained how we conducted business, and one of the new group asked the faculty member to explain why we did things that way. I had been in the department long enough to know that the new guy had just pounded the first nail in his coffin. I predicted he would not last beyond his first year, and unfortunately, I was right. I am not sure he realized what he was doing to himself, which is regrettable, or how welcome his refreshing perspective really was to me. His comment made me feel part of the problem. — Abby

Durkheim (1953) defined the collective conscience of a group as their normative orientation or what they agree to follow. Culture is about the shared meanings that people have that affect how they relate to one another (Eagleton, 2000). Culture is the professional culture, the shared meanings of what college and university faculty experience as they explore the life of the mind.

It's amazing that I found time to get my work done. During my first couple of years in higher ed, I was told to be careful so as to "sidestep the land mines." Then I needed to be quiet and learn where the "bodies were buried" so I wouldn't make the same mistakes they evidently made. I could never figure out how some colleagues had the time to undermine my work when there were only twenty-four hours in a day. — Abby

---

Each profession has its own set of customs, acceptable behaviors, symbols, and means of social control. One component that distinguishes professional culture is the confirmation of power that usually flows from professional expertise. The power of the professional culture is manifest in the service or expertise that the professional group provides. Besides learning the profession, a neophyte must also master what Vollmer and Mills (1966) labeled "the labyrinth of the professional culture" (p. 18). They declared that "community welfare would be immeasurably impaired by its absence" (p. 16). In addition, they characterized the professional career role as conveying a certain attitude that demonstrates affinity for or a calling to the professional career versus a desire for selfish motives. Therefore, adjustment through acculturation must be complete. Vollmer and Mills labeled colleagues who do not acculturate successfully "deviant, . . . peculiar, unorthodox, annoying, . . . or trouble-maker" (p. 18). In other words, not everyone admitted into a professional culture always upholds the values of the culture, especially if their motivation is more self-serving than altruistic and communal. To be viewed as a member of the profession, however, may prompt some members to act outwardly and superficially in accordance with prevailing cultural values while performing troubling behaviors beneath the observable surface. Bullies often shroud their machinations in secrecy. Thus, academic culture harbors open as well as secret compartments.

Academic Culture Defined

Goffman (1959) described a culture as one whose outer appearance or front region is friendly, cooperative, presentable, and marketable. However, the unseen portions of the culture are often ambiguous and cluttered, with back regions purposefully hidden from view.

This perspective describes academic culture effectively. In fact, while institutional mission and philosophy shape academic culture, the symbolic translation of these ideals into practice shapes what faculty and administrators do and how they act (Fairweather, 2002; Gould, 2003). Theoretically, espoused academic beliefs and practices should closely align with daily academic practices (Dennison, 1990; Schein, 1992). However, cultural reality is also laced with faculty and administrative egos, hidden agendas, done deals, ideological conflicts, personality clashes, and power struggles (Fairweather, 2000; Seldin, 1984). Some of these are visible on the surface, as Goffman indicated. But bullies can lie dormant, hidden from view and ready to erupt.

Incumbent faculty expect their new colleagues to be socialized into the academic culture. Some are clearly assisted in that process, but others are not. Hiring practices that follow homosocial reproduction principles extend employment to colleagues like themselves, which tends to make the socialization process pro forma. In the past few decades, the emerging faculty candidate pool has become less homogeneous and less like the previously existing pool, rendering the socialization process more tenuous.

In fact, faculty who do not socialize themselves to the nuances of the academic culture may be simultaneously blissful and doomed. More important, faculty must learn how the university and academic culture functions in order to know if they are being bullied (Zemsky, Wegner, & Massy, 2005).

The culture of research in academe may be fodder for bullying. When faculty see rewards forthcoming for research, they are likely to allocate or reallocate their time and energy. The staunchest faculty supporters of research are not likely to embrace easily a reallocation of their time to teaching and service. They will likely stall the organizational structure and hold tightly to the prevailing academic research culture to thwart any attempts to modify work expectations. For their part, new faculty may willingly embrace the change because they have not yet had an opportunity to acclimate to the culture of research. This situation highlights an ongoing battle waged by faculty who support the culture of research versus those who do not (Finkelstein, Seal, & Schuster, 1998). Each is trying to preserve what he or she does best in the face of impeding or impending cultural change. This has implications for the future of a department because it affects the hiring and socializing of new faculty (Lang, 2005).

Tierney (1997) distinguished between modern and postmodern perspectives on how faculty are socialized into the academic role. In the more linear, modernist philosophy, socialization is a unitary process, defined by the academic culture and reinforced by those doing the socializing. The modernist acknowledges that behavior is learned behavior and passed on to succeeding members. In the postmodernist view, culture is constructed rather than simply passed down. Postmodernists assume that incumbents can mold culture, that is, that culture responds to different voices and perspectives. In terms of understanding incivility and bullying, are people acting uncivil in order to short-cut or circumvent the system to get ahead or simply to wield power by bullying to accomplish a desired personal end?

Culture should evolve. However, tension and change spawn uncertainty and instability. Uncertainty widens and deepens as a result of the time lag between discussion and implementation and subsequent acceptance of the change within the culture. Owen and Demb (2004) noted that "with the unsettling nature of transformational change, which challenges assumptions, roles, values, and norms, participants experience a disturbing lack of control and the result is a situation full of both personal and institutional tensions" (p. 658). One reason is that the academic culture usually changes at a glacial pace. Owen and Demb indicated the introduction of dysfunction to the system, causing faculty to respond in counterproductive ways, including incivility, bullying, and mobbing.

Consider this trend in academe. Zemsky, Wegner, and Massy (2005) contended that faculty disengage from the university in response to administrative tactics aimed at change. With the increase in the research function, universities have outsourced classroom teaching duties to adjuncts and part-timers. The results are fewer tenure-track positions, more part-time positions, tighter job mobility, greater administrative intrusiveness on faculty autonomy, less faculty involvement in campus governance, increases in bureaucracy, splintered disciplines, lower morale, increased workloads, and decreased rewards (Austin & Gamson, 1983)—in other words, a tense, changing culture.

Zemsky, Wagner, and Massy (2005) realized, however, that administrators must "balance the traditions of the academy against the demands of the market" (p. 51). Therefore, dissatisfied full-time faculty stand against administrators who propose and push for change while preserving quality or touting excellence as a vision statement. Other full-time faculty, by contrast, view the market forces as opportunities to push their own research agendas through entrepreneurial means such as marketing inventions and discoveries (Slaughter, Archerd, & Campbell, 2004). Because administrators are more likely to favor anything that decreases costs and increases revenues, they are likely to see the merits generated by the entrepreneurial faculty. Unfortunately, this group may be more inwardly than altruistically focused, creating a divide with nonentrepreneurial faculty. Once again we see the battle of cosmopolitans versus locals (Gouldner, 1957, 1958). In any case, market forces (the cosmopolitans) are pitted against the university mission that a core group of faculty (the locals) strives to preserve at all cost. If the locals are unable to preserve the existing academic culture, they are likely to retreat into their disciplinary silos or try to bully their way through the evolving system (Newman, Couturier, & Scurry, 2004; Zemsky, Wegner, & Massy, 2005).

Intellectual Climate and Academic Freedom Challenged

College faculty have been characterized as quirky, eccentric, and absent-minded. Unexpected behaviors are considered normal to the insider in addition to being thought simply odd to any outsider (Dziech & Weiner, 1990). This is part of the unique intellectual climate that emerges from a romanticized academic culture. The degree to which a faculty member is stimulated within an intellectual climate to be productive, however, often hedges on colleague-to-colleague interaction and support (Hermanowicz, 2005). For instance, high intellectual climates generate a higher scholarly production of books, grants, articles, and conference presentations. If the institution values and rewards teaching, faculty are more likely to want to improve their teaching skills (Blackburn & Lawrence, 1995; Finkelstein, 1997; Menges & Weimer, 1996). But not all individuals within the culture may value what the culture values; therefore, conflict and dysfunction can harbor a resulting intellectual climate of isolation, indecision, and dissension. Change and transformation can spawn conflict (Dahrendorf, 1958). In the face of change, new faculty look to see who and what is being rewarded and will probably pursue those paths because they too want to be rewarded, promoted, and tenured. Having to make these shifts and adjustments may produce tension among faculty. Some will seek external outlets for rewards, but these may be counterproductive to the institutional mission, the intellectual climate, and the academic culture (Blackburn & Lawrence, 1995).

When faculty place themselves on the job market, they must compete fiercely with others, so research products act as cultural capital or totem and have become highly valued (Legislative Office of Education Oversight, 1993). Faculty members who are less adept and successful at research and grant writing take on the role of second-class citizens and will be hired only at second- or third-tier institutions. In other words, they have little totem or exchange value in an academic marketplace that values research-oriented collateral. These colleagues are treated differently from others.

In yet another challenge, although academic freedom was designed to protect scholarly pursuits, the reality is that specialists within disciplines bicker, departments jockey for prominence within a college, and individual faculty members hang on to long-standing bitterness toward certain colleagues (see Lang, 2005). Faculty hold academic freedom sacred, because to stifle research and scholarship or teaching behaviors would potentially squelch research. But academic culture has tended to say, in essence, "If you leave me alone to do my agenda, I will leave you to do yours. If I can be anonymous, I will tell you exactly what I think and feel, but if I must be identified, my stance will be neutral lest I or my work be the target of the next inquiry." Administrators and faculty colleagues probably will not venture outside their academic culture comfort zone to become involved in another's business because to do so would "violate group autonomy" (Dziech & Weiner, 1990, p. 48).

Collegiality and the Community of Scholars

Bode (1996) defined *collegiality* as equal power vested in colleagues. Collegiality may be present in theory but usually is rare in practice. Some faculty regard collegiality as the support system they share with other faculty. However, each academic department supports varying degrees of collegiality as perceived by each faculty member, such that equal power is not vested in all members of a community of scholars. To determine the extent to which new faculty perceive collegiality as more social or more scholarly, Bode found most faculty members rated their department as average in collegiality. Characteristics of such departments deemed average in collegiality included some sense of community, social support, and informal interactions with colleagues. Highly collegial departments, by contrast, have a more pronounced sense of intellectual support, collaborative interaction, and extensive involvement with colleagues. Newer faculty may be unaware of expectations colleagues have of them or share the same philosophical stance as seasoned faculty or understand what is expected of them collegially. In fact, "competition has replaced collegiality" (Blackburn & Lawrence, 1995, p. 3).

Collegiality may be masking behaviors that have manifested themselves as normative (Hoel & Salin, 2003; Zapf & Einarsen, 2003) but nevertheless undermine the academic culture. Bergquist (1992) said that the presence of a strong administration means that the collegial culture is perhaps weak and competing for survival in the organization. Faculty may manifest their resistance in unnoticeable but myriad ways (Eagleton, 2000; Hoel & Salin; Zapf & Einarsen, 2003). Given faculty intellectual prowess and professional expertise (Eagleton, 2000), these subsequent social acts could appear sinister and complicit (Said, 1993). Bergquist noted that this rise in a faculty negotiating culture serves to reclaim much of the loss experienced by a disenfranchised faculty struggling to maneuver in a strong administrative environment. Bullying used as political strategy could be a means to regain lost ground.

Unfortunately, attempts to increase faculty cultural capital through the use of negotiation and micropolitics go unnoticed or are inadvertently tolerated and rewarded (Diamond, 1993; Hoel, Einarsen, & Cooper, 2003; Zapf & Einarsen, 2003). Based on changes and undue stress on the traditional academic culture, these institutional survival-of-the-fittest norms may inadvertently encourage aggressive behaviors (Hoel & Salin, 2003; Neuman & Baron, 2003). These may be exacerbated by the introduction of precipitating forces. They may also be supported consciously or unconsciously by faculty and administrators. Furthermore, social control mechanisms in place in academe work silently and invisibly, and effectively, so that new faculty regulate their behavior to conform to the prevailing academic norms of the institution (Baez, 2002), be they positive or negative.

The institution is religious, patriarchal, and the women should be seen and not heard, not be noticed. Women treat each other badly given this culture. I thought they would band together to help each other, but it was interesting to see how they treated women who spoke up. They would say, "Don't do that because it will be bad for the rest of us." These women were the best disciplinarians or guardians of the culture. There was a fear of upsetting the balance. — Caroline

---

Camouflaged aggression used as a social control mechanism and also to secure scarce resources and status not only goes undetected; it may be culturally accepted. In fact, some faculty, some departments, or some administrators sanction it under the guise of autonomy and academic freedom. Peyton (2003) suggested that when incivility and bullying are permitted to prevail in the academic culture, they may have been created and supported by the managers and administrators overseeing the organization.

I recall an administrator [a dean] questioning my intelligence because I didn't agree with him . . . [receiving] open criticism in hallways and other public areas . . . and on several occasions not receiving support for proposals [he] handled in a dismissive manner and unprofessional fashion, on two occasions followed by an incredulous statement to a secretary or assistant followed by a little laughter. — George

Someone did go to the dean and complain about a chair, but the dean said that as long as they don't go over the budget, there is no problem. He did not want to get involved in how the department was managed. — Lucille

---

For instance, a supervisor may withhold merit increases unfairly and without substantial and objective explanation during faculty end-of-the-year performance evaluations (Peyton, 2003) in order to control a faculty member who is not following normative expectations. These types of evaluations could be exacerbating the problem because what is expected of faculty goes largely unwritten and understated (Clark & Corcoran, 1986). Thus, negative actions and decisions may go undetected, unreported, and unpunished because they are difficult to harness and prove. Furthermore, according to Tierney (2004), "tenure has become not a structure to protect the ideal but one that corrupts it" (p. 167).

Rayner, Hoel, and Cooper (2002) contended that if a culture harbors passive-aggressive and bullying behavior, a change in culture can diminish or eliminate these aggressive, dysfunctional behaviors. Unfortunately, tenured faculty who bully cannot be terminated as easily as administrators can, and the latter may simply return to their faculty positions and continue being aggressors (Ferris, 2004). The status quo is often maintained.

Social World and Social Knowledge

Traditionally we differentiate institutions of higher education based on concrete aspects such as size, selectivity, structure, and support, but we tend to overlook the cultural similarities and dissimilarities of institutions. How faculty construct their social world in the department, school, and university determines the academic cultural context (Berger & Luckman, 1967). This sociocultural environment in turn explains faculty behavior, frames reality, and socializes new entrants and incumbents (Hermanowicz, 2005). Hermanowicz maintained that the organizational structure and the academic culture are interactive but often uphold differing viewpoints or realities on matters or issues.

Social knowledge refers to how faculty perceive their work environment. It includes what the institution values (teaching, research, or service, ambition, commitment, collegiality, and integrity) and how one perceives other faculty colleagues and the administration's competence and supportiveness. Faculty form that social knowledge "from experiences with colleagues, administrators, committee decisions, faculty meetings, institutional rules and norms, and professional association practices" (Blackburn & Lawrence, 1995, p. 99). Especially important is the knowledge of what is rewarded, which becomes part of faculty members' behavioral repertoire, motivating them to use rewarded behaviors. In addition, as part of their social learning process, faculty members are motivated and guided by feedback on their behavioral choices and how closely they adhere to the normative standard acceptable for that department.

Self-determination appreciably affects one's motivation to learn in accordance with social norms. Intrinsic motivation is more important than extrinsic motivation to learned behavior. Given that academic culture traditionally has supported knowledge for knowledge's sake in pursuit of idealistic and altruistic goals, faculty behavior over the years has likely been motivated by intrinsic needs (Guiffrida, 2006). Job involvement theory (Herzberg, Mausner, & Snyderman, 1959; Kanungo, 1982) posits how one's socially and culturally intrinsic and extrinsic needs and motivations affect the way one involves oneself in the job. For instance, the power of extrinsic rewards such as merit pay, opportunity for promotion and tenure, and opportunity for advancement to administrative positions may increase involvement in one's job, especially if intrinsic needs are being met elsewhere. These extrinsic rewards have become more motivating in a gradually changing academic culture. However, faculty left with the prospect of only intrinsic rewards may affect the intellectual climate in adverse ways. Rosenzweig (1998) regards faculty members as "badly fractured" as their "loyalties are divided among their disciplines, their corporate affiliations, their research sponsors, and finally, their students, and their institutions" (pp. 105–106). These divisions pull faculty in opposite directions.

In a qualitative study of sixty physicists in top-, middle-, and lower-tier doctoral research institutions, Hermanowicz (2005) identified the effect that each type of academic culture has on the prevailing intellectual climate. His study of physicists, in a pure discipline atop the scientific hierarchy, provided him an opportunity to examine the similarities and differences of norms governing academic behavior within each of these tiered social worlds. He noted the top tier had expectations for performance and recognition and a research imperative to achieve elite status within the physics community. Low-tier social worlds emphasized teaching and good departmental citizenship. Middle-tier departments straddled research and teaching. Clearly in the elite tier, expectations for research and scholarship in physics leading to career eminence were expected, socialized for, and rewarded. Failure to deliver such expectations resulted in admonishment, failure, degradation, isolation, or no tenure or promotion.

Clear boundaries were drawn in the physics community such that each department knew where it stood in the pecking order (Hermanowicz, 2005). Middle-tier hopefuls placed themselves in tenuous positions trying to emulate the top-tier elite, having academic power over the lowest tier but never quite penetrating the guarded elite boundary of the top-tier departments. Middle-tier faculty members rationalized that elitist programs harbored egos, turf battles, dishonesty, and cutthroat politics and professed themselves happy in the middle. The lower-tier institutions could not change the elitism of the top tier, and the top tier saw no reason to change because they probably saw no problem with their behavior or the ranking system.

Becher and Trowler (2001) posited that eminence is a precursor to power. For instance, eminent professors are more likely to exercise power over professors at the bottom of the hierarchy who have not yet amassed the human, social, and cultural capital necessary for eminence. Peer review processes uphold these standards and values as well as the means to or for eminence or the validation of it. However, peer review systems within the culture are not devoid of politics, political agenda setting, posturing, sloppy oversight, and procedural problems. Therefore, normative standards may shift based on the committee of peers (a subset of a community of scholars) doing the reviewing, and there is no doubt that academe harbors less-than-good citizens.

Social Worlds and Faculty Turf Battles

Each faculty member possesses a slightly different philosophy. Disagreements stemming from these differences can include anything from teaching mode to research agenda topics to research paradigm used. Faculty may also differ on policy and rule interpretation, its repercussions, and its effects on others. Perceived isolation may delude faculty into thinking that their individual actions and disagreements do not affect or harm others at the university (Dziech & Weiner, 1990). Furthermore, the fine line between ethical and unethical is often blurry. While some behaviors can be attributed to or explained by academic freedom, other behaviors might fall within the realm of incompetence, incivility, or harassment. This may be based on who is challenging whom, when, where, and about what. Moreover, the social world within the academic culture is passed on to the next generation of faculty, perhaps along with those turf battles. This is especially true of full-time students, who see and hear what is going on in departments (Weidman, Twale, & Stein, 2001). How they see faculty behaving is likely to be part of their socialization process as doctoral students and then perhaps continued as they join a faculty department on the tenure track.

Interviews in Golde's study of science and humanities students who departed early from their programs (2005) as opposed to staying revealed that students often left because their expectations differed from the department's normative standards and practices. In some cases, it was difficult for students to acclimate well to the academic culture, in part because faculty did not assist them effectively in the acculturation and socialization processes. Golde's data revealed that attrition also resulted from peer and faculty isolation. As a result, doctoral students were not likely to participate in supportive relationships or see and experience the positive aspects of collegiality. Learning and being socialized into the academic culture is a formal and informal process that begins in graduate school (Weidman, Twale, & Stein, 2001) and continues for junior faculty.

There is no way to know if students are being formally or informally socialized by faculty mentors and dissertation chairs to practice collegiality, collaboration, and cooperative behavior (Abdennur, 2000; Coyne, Craig, & Smith-Lee Chong, 2004; Gayle, Bhoendradatt, & White, 2003; Peyton, 2003; Smith, Singer, Hoel, & Cooper, 2003; White, 2004). Do graduate students witness the lack of collegiality being practiced and rewarded as they proceed through their doctoral program? Are they being purposefully shielded from it, to their detriment? Because culture is passed to subsequent generations of students, what aspects are being passed to new scholars? If incivility is permitted, the new members will absorb it as normative. Departments are communicating to graduate students that bullying is acceptable and perhaps even rewarded, and passing this information along to the next generation of faculty. Being treated uncivilly and bullied by colleagues may be perceived by newer and untenured faculty members as a rite of passage deemed necessary for success in the profession. As a result it becomes tolerated and ingrained (Schein, 1992).

Part II

Pinpointing Causes

Systemic change, or the threat of it, is likely to fuel aggressive behavior in any workplace. Broad and sometimes unanticipated social and economic changes threaten to alter the prevailing academic institution, its organizational structure, and, most important, its traditions and culture. Any transformation will likely be met with resistance from incumbents. Two ongoing pressure points to the academic status quo that may be illuminating, and exacerbating, faculty incivility, camouflaged aggression, bullying, and mobbing are the changing face of academe and the corporate redefinition of an education (Newman, Couturier, & Scurry, 2004). Regardless, faculty still prefer to be empowered and equitably treated by administration and colleagues (Newman, Couturier, & Scurry, 2004; Washburn, 2005).

The anticipated changes in store for higher education portend a turbulent future, and what it holds for faculty is nothing short of transformation. These imposed changes go deeper into the fabric of the academy because they involve political struggles between peers for the values they challenge and the struggles they impose over scarce resources. The very presence of new groups challenges centuries-old traditions. The chapters in Part Two capture the motivating, enabling, and precipitating pressures and forces in the conceptual framework that point to an increase in incivility, bullying, and workplace aggression.

6

The Changing Face of Academe as a Precipitating Circumstance

[The entry of women in academe] represented at best an unwelcome intrusion and at worst a serious threat to men committed to the life of the mind.
                    Billie Wright Dziech and Linda Weiner

People of color were perceived as threats.
                    Gail Thompson and Angela Louque

Most outsiders to academe believe the university is a serene environment where scholars pursue a life of the mind. In fact, for some, academe is likely to be chilly, unreceptive, limiting, and contentious. The professoriat for the most part has been dominated by white males. Historically, women and minorities have been vulnerable groups in academe. These groups are more likely to assume nontenure-track, adjunct, or part-time appointments and lower salaries; encounter negative promotion and tenure decisions; and disproportionately find themselves token appointees to committees. Subtle harassment occurs through nonconfrontational, institutionalized acts of standard practice that favor traditional groups over the newer entrants.

Incentives to diversify the academy over the past several decades have created more of a battleground than a harmonious, inviting workplace. Those who once enjoyed power, authority, and respect among the old guard may see an erosion of that power with the introduction of new gender and ethnic groups. Natural events such as additions and departures, dissents, stalemates, upheavals, and overthrows happen within a culture, but as with any other denigrating forces or political or economic challenges, there is an equal and opposite challenge to stifle the ensuing problem. Unfortunately, academic culture holds onto its staunchest members, emotionally and ideologically. Members are free to change and go elsewhere, but the need to belong and preserve the academic status quo is overwhelming (Eagleton, 2000). Thus, faculty may resort to unusual behaviors in order to ensure that preservation. In some instances, white male faculty resistance has marginalized women and minority groups in academe. Because higher education tends to find itself adjusting to changing circumstances at a glacial pace (Altbach & Finkelstein, 1997), the mere visibility of diverse groups does not guarantee their immediate acceptance (Aquirre, 2000; Bloom, 1987; D'Souza, 1991).

The introduction of women and minority faculty in academe began with the "chilly climate" of the 1970s. Some authors and researchers would argue that the temperature has risen slightly but not enough over the past thirty years to warm that chill. This climate is one of the two precipitating factors that has had an effect on the academic culture and the increases of incivility. Solomon (1989) characterized women and minorities who entered academe as lacking "material well-being, power, and prestige" (p. 644). The result has been their oppression. A historical look at the diversification of the once fairly homogeneous academe is followed by a discussion of issues of inequality, tokenism, and marginalization to establish the changing face of academe as a precipitating factor for faculty incivility and the rise of an academic bully culture.

The Changing Face of Academe

Historically a homogeneous academic culture remained unchallenged, but the entrance of new and underrepresented groups raised issues that majority incumbents had never considered issues before

(Brubaker & Rudy, 1997). Academic structures had been designed, controlled, and administrated by men (Hadikin & O'Driscoll, 2000). Slow, minimal progress for women academics occurred between 1972 and 1984 (Etaugh, 1984). However, thirty years ago, women with advanced degrees experienced more job tension. In a study of full-time community college faculty, Hollon and Gemmill (1976) found that women participated less in decision making, experienced greater job-related tension and less job involvement, and had lower overall job satisfaction than men did. They also reported having less power than men and thus less of a part in decision-making activities. Thirty years ago, Clark's analysis (1977) indicated that women were excluded in academe in communication networks, social invitations, committee assignments, and projects. What was labeled then as discrimination still remains; the difference is that it is more subtle now.

Twenty years ago Clark and Corcoran (1986) wrote that women were largely excluded and considered suspect based on their gender in terms of how they threatened male colleagues. Women were not always evaluated based on their ability. Thus, women found themselves hitting the glass ceiling when they sought advancement. They also noted that female graduate students and minority students, both women and men, encountered barriers to their success. Women and minorities may have been overlooked for the best positions or the best institutions, and even when they were hired, they were excluded from full participation in academe.

In a study of faculty, Finkelstein, Seal, and Schuster (1998) found that increases in numbers of women academics occurred across all fields and that fields that were traditionally male were hiring more women and, to a lesser extent, faculty of color. Although 80 percent of new faculty reported overall career satisfaction, their level of satisfaction appeared slightly below that of senior faculty. The authors concluded that the major concerns of faculty were job security and salary.

Inequality and Inequity

The demographic composition of the faculty has changed. Schuster and Finkelstein (2006) report that 36 percent of faculty are now female and 14 percent are nonwhite. Forty-four percent of new entrants are women, 20 percent are nonwhite, and 18 percent are foreign born. Their study showed that although the professoriat in general reports the presence of workplace equity, women and nonwhite faculty do not. In other words, women faculty and faculty of color do not feel that they are treated equitably or equally. Ironically, white males perceive that women and nonwhites are being treated equitably. Nevertheless, more women than men accepted positions off the tenure track and were more likely to be part time. One could question whether these preferences are female affinities or subtle attempts at marginalization.

Although there have been increases in women and minority students and faculty in academe, these groups still encounter "social and structural hurdles" (Blackburn & Lawrence, 1995, p. 43). Paternalism and subsequent workplace dominant or subordinate relationships remain as residuals to sustain what Miller (1986) referred to as "permanent inequality." She pondered, "What do people do to people who are different from them?" (p. 222) and responded that perhaps they behave in unanticipated ways, possibly through incivility or bullying. This, coupled with patriarchy, renders certain historically subordinate groups natural victims (Hoel, Faragher, & Cooper, 2004; Jennifer, Cowie, & Ananiadou, 2003).

Furthermore, new entrants and underrepresented groups are placed in conflict with prevailing cultural norms and potentially hostile authority figures in the organizational structure. Tierney and Bensimon (1996) argued that incumbent members of an academic institution see that institution from only one perspective even though new entrants offer multiple perspectives. Because the dominant workplace group dictates culture and normative behavior, the subordinate groups can observe and respond only as subordinates, much as they do outside the workplace, that is, passively. Members of the dominant group act dominantly because they always have, both in and outside the workplace, so they see their behavior as normal, if not as benevolently paternalistic. Faculty are paternalistic (Bergquist, 1992). Subordinates may or may not see it that way, but they nevertheless are often obliging and accepting and less likely to take risks or cause conflict to change matters radically. Morrison and von Glinow (1990) noted that the differential treatment in the workplace hiring of subordinate groups by dominant ones had less to do with job fitness and more to do with a trade-off to satisfy quotas or simply to window-dress. This mechanism treats women and minorities unfairly and provides fertile ground for uncivil behaviors and bullying through unequal, overt supervisory relationships or discrepancies in faculty status and rank.

One year I recall a junior professor presented his credentials for tenure in his fourth year rather than his fifth. This sparked a lively debate among the tenured departmental faculty in attendance. You could tell the old guard was resistant on principle of having this upstart get tenure early. No one had been able to do that before. His file was really very good, but they offered dissenting explanations in the meeting like, "We support him, but we are concerned with how it will look up the line," meaning at the university committee level. "Faculty have two attempts to get tenure here, and he could be blowing one of them. We don't want to see him hurt or disappointed if they don't think he is as good as we do." The big debate was over the tenure document wording that the candidate must be "outstanding" to be considered in the fourth year. That was the criterion they used to justify their resistance, even though I could tell they were just being paternalistic. If he didn't ask for their permission ahead of time, they weren't going to grant him entrance into the club. — Abby

---

However, years of observation place subordinates in a perfect position to challenge the dominant group. Unfortunately, their internalization of the expected passive response renders subordinates as victims and unlikely risk takers who would be willing to challenge prevailing norms and dominant group members (Miller, 1995). Miller (1986) illustrated that the frustration between the groups manifests itself in destructive behaviors such that peers treat each other maliciously. Interestingly, subordinates who want to be dominant diligently play the game but rarely gain acceptance into the dominant group.

According to Miller (1986), each cultural tradition emphasizes certain specific and different human behaviors and awards them some degree of importance. Over time some behaviors become highly valued and part of the repertoire used by those who hold dominant roles. Acceptance of these behaviors as significant and important by those who dominate means that other behaviors are dismissed or relegated to a lesser position so the new behaviors could be mastered. Miller believed that because males dominate most cultures, their behaviors have gained more acceptance than female behaviors, which have more recently entered the workforce. By the same token, females have learned the behaviors associated with their subordinate role because they grew up in a patriarchal society.

Women understand being victimized and have developed coping strategies. Men, in contrast, grew up training for and mastering the dominant position. Therefore, they experience greater difficulty with their own weaknesses and may lash out at female and minority coworkers who have the potential to identify and to bring to the light those weaknesses. Miller (1986) believes this gives birth to incivility in the form of passive victimization through marginalization and tokenism and indicates why men more than women bully others.

Passive Victimization

When women entered higher education in greater numbers after World War II, they situated themselves or were situated by incumbents in the entry-level ranks at lower pay. Challenging the power structure posed its own problems for women, many of whom were new to academe and unlikely to know the academic culture or the subtle nuances of the academic organization or governance structure (Dziech & Weiner, 1990). Depending on from where they came—places such as public schools, business, industry, hospitals, or social agencies—new female entrants were heavily steeped in a different culture and had difficulty desocializing and then resocializing into academe (Weidman, Twale, & Stein, 2001). Some newcomers did not realize they had to change, others did not know how to change or learned too late how to adapt, and others defied or challenged what they saw. This last group attempted to impose their workplace culture of origin onto the centuries-old academic culture, but to no avail. As a result, these pioneering women were "recruited grudgingly, regarded with suspicion, treated like intruders, and reviewed cynically" (Dziech & Weiner, p. 57). They were bullied.

Glazer-Raymo (1999) also noted changes in the workforce when women entered. She said questions arose as to whether women were already being victimized in the workplace as a result of their receiving lower wages and having lower status than male counterparts. Women's initial entry into academe appeared more discipline specific, but over the years it has expanded to include more disciplines and professional fields. And since the early 1990s, the enrollment of women at all educational levels has exceeded male enrollment. However, degree attainment, especially the doctorate, still favors male graduates. Women of color account for one-fourth of women at all levels of education, and they earn fewer degrees than men of color earn. In certain fields that are now considered feminized—education, humanities, and psychology—women prevail in number of doctorates awarded. Despite the feminization of certain fields, many are at the lower ranks, while the senior ranks and administration remain predominantly male (see also Lomperis, 1990).

What effect does the feminization of a field have on academic cultural change in that field as well as on attitudes and instances of incivility by men? Glazer-Raymo (1999) believes that the simple presence of women and minorities in proportionate or predominant numbers has camouflaged what may really be happening: passive aggression meted out through lower salaries, lower status, tokenism, and fewer opportunities for advancement. Glazer-Raymo referred to the dual inequity track that legitimizes a lower status for women across higher education. Men make up the senior faculty ranks, but fewer than half of women are on the tenure track, placing them at a decided disadvantage in policy matters and decision making. More women work part time in academe and find themselves as adjuncts, postdoctoral fellows, and employees on limited contracts due to nonrenewable soft money grants, which serves to create an underclass of lower-paid individuals. Given these circumstances, women are often treated as second-class citizens and remain dispensable. Women also believe their treatment in the academic workplace is less than fair compared to how men are treated. Women and minorities have become contributing academics but often remain part of the invisible workers who offer much-appreciated cost savings to institutions. These groups, when working full time, are also tapped to serve as representatives on service committees for which little recognition or reward is given but much time is expended.

In their study of female natural and social scientists, Settles, Cortina, Malley, and Stewart (2006) found that due to work climate, female social scientists were more likely to be satisfied with their faculty position than were women in the natural sciences.

They reasoned that the natural sciences departments were more male dominated and there was a greater likelihood of gender discrimination or a sexist climate.

Newer faculty, particularly women and minorities, tended to ask more personal and socially relevant questions that challenged what academics had long been led to believe. These newer voices challenged the previous research done solely by and about white male populations. Unfortunately, the academy, governed by peer review, dictated that the old guard faculty judge and reward the new faculty, based on traditional norms and scholarship that often favor old epistemologies. Once again women and minority voices have the potential to become restricted, marginalized, or ignored. Braskamp and Wergin (1998) noted that academic values still affect institutional citizenship, but the changing face of academe designed to promote the public good through diversity and inclusion challenges the existing academic culture and structure.

Tokenism

When new groups of people, such as ethnic minorities or women, began entering academia, they were, and often still are, called tokens. Tokens challenge the norms of a patriarchal system and face myriad problems. The isolation associated with tokenism causes declining self-image and self-esteem and eventual exit. Tokenism in itself serves as a teaser, an unstated promise that more tokens, like the first token, will be hired and because the tokens are so well suited for the position, promotion is indeed a possibility (Yoder, 1985). Both are unlikely. Multiple tokens will change the system over time, disrupting the status quo, but there is no real guarantee that equity or equality will result. However, incivility might.

According to Kanter (1977), the introduction of someone different into a culture causes the dominant group members to be more self-conscious about their greater numbers and conscious of why they are the dominant group. As a result, token individuals live and work under a microscope that is filtered through a cultural lens. Symbolically, dominant groups observe and judge to see how these newer entrants perform new roles in the new culture and how in their new roles they fulfill the images or stereotypes of the cultural group they represent. If they fail to live up to expectation, they are eliminated, treated uncivilly, bullied, taken advantage of, or marginalized.

Kanter (1977) noted why token placements can easily be victimized in the organization. New groups to academe are asked to represent the organization on committees as token members. They have become stereotyped and judged against a false or unachievable standard. Their presence on the committee might convey a false sense of authority or importance, if not likability or validation. Unfortunately, their visibility subsequently renders them unsuspecting targets of aggression.

Dominance, Subordination, and Marginalization

Academe is a unique culture where by virtue of credential, faculty with doctorates would be presumed to have dominant status in the academic culture. Miller (1986) noted several decades ago that increasing numbers of this dominant culture have been women who have traditionally held a subordinate status in society. This may have its advantages as well as obvious disadvantages. Those in subordinate positions can observe dominant behavior, which can be advantageous for them.

Women have done a great deal of observation of the male role in society long before they seek the doctorate or work in academe. They are raised and socialized to cooperate, whereas men are encouraged to compete. Those dynamics change when women are hired into traditionally male roles. The competition begins, but the game takes on some interesting twists. When men try to dominate women in the academic workplace, women, whether they realize it or not, nevertheless have an advantage.

They have probably been dominated in some manner or fashion outside academe long before they entered it and have observed the dominant culture in action without realizing what they have learned as a result. They were outsiders looking in as young girls and teenagers. Men who are dominated have not necessarily been privy to the same observations because they were on the inside, training to be the dominators. To survive as a subordinate in a dominant culture, one must, according to Miller (1986), change and revise one's individual psychological makeup. It is not enough simply to mimic members of the dominant culture and simultaneously dissociate oneself from the subordinate culture. Subordinate culture members are in a position to learn the dominant role more effectively than they realize and use coping strategies they have learned in the past to succeed in an uncivil environment. Unfortunately, women and academics of color probably do not realize this position as good fortune that they can use to their advantage.

Kanter (1977) posited that when subordinates try to assert their power and authority, only to have it blocked, they will seek power over those whom they can dominate. Usually that power is directed downward in the hierarchy. She said, "People respond to the restrictiveness of their own situation by behaving restrictively toward others" (p. 189). This may be accomplished with newer groups entering academe because they are perceived by others to be powerless or in precarious positions within the hierarchy. If faculty lower in the pecking order fail to conform to social norms and standards, the individuals may be isolated or rendered powerless and find themselves working in an inhospitable academic environment. Where stakes are higher and reputation is important, competition and pressure to succeed are also greater. Unfortunately, faculty elites may not always adhere to a moral career because "their commitment and identification is socially controlled by those with whom they work" (Hermanowicz, 2005, p. 43).

Marginalization of Minority Groups

Minority women hired into historically white male disciplines or professions where an imbalance in gender and race already exists are particularly vulnerable. Once these academics survive the incivility, they have little energy to assist other contemporaries in similar struggles, although they tend to be supportive and empathetic. Self-preservation by helping another colleague may prove counterproductive, however. Fear of repercussions for mounting the cause could prove equally or more debilitating than dealing with the bully or the original uncivil incident (Dziech & Weiner, 1990).

Thompson and Louque (2005) reported that disrespect for African American faculty stemmed from some colleagues' lack of knowledge about black culture in general as well as a slight lack of respect for African Americans' academic contributions and their professional opinions. In a survey of African American faculty, they found that 60 percent of the respondents reported being marginalized, and half indicated that happened frequently. They acknowledged that "people of color were perceived as threats" (p. 95). Also emerging from their research was the finding that "hidden agendas cannot tolerate public exposure" (p. 95). Each of these findings limited participation by women and minorities. In other words, there is a tendency for dominant groups to marginalize subordinate groups in subtle and covert ways. However, the reverse is also possible.

This great job became available, and I was fortunate to have an interview. The last session of the day was with the African American dean. As she invited me into the office, she turned on her CD player, turned up the volume, and shut the door. I thought she was setting the mood. As I sat down, she told me I had an impressive vita and then asked what my agenda was. I thought she was referring to my research agenda, so I told her what it was. Her disparaging expression was enough to know that I gave the wrong answer. Then she proceeded to tell me a story of the downfall of a well-known operatic diva and asked me what happens to divas and tyrants. I was stunned and speechless. She then said tyrants are killed or banished to the fringes. The next twenty minutes were unbearable both because of what she was doing to me unnecessarily and because I knew I would never get that job. — Abby

---

Marginalization of Academic Work

Promotion and tenure, admissions, and graduate faculty status documents, among others, developed by academic communities of scholars may harbor passive aggression. Hart (2006) posited a feminist framework for her document analysis that claimed male-centered dominance was indeed coupled with female oppression. However, she claimed that in spite of patriarchy in academic culture, women still succeeded even though marginalization still prevailed for some. Normative expectations for status in the professoriat were tied to scholarly publication in refereed outlets. Of importance was not only where a piece was published but what new knowledge was published. Therefore, feminist studies were less likely to appear in mainstream or top-tier journals, so alternative venues and outlets were established for such scholarship. These alternatives had marginal status, however, regardless of how substantial or pertinent the research. In Hart's study of the three top higher education administration journals, she noted a greater presence of women among the journal authors; however, feminist scholarship did not have the same presence. This indicated perhaps that it had been marginalized, because less than 1 percent of the articles in the past twelve years had addressed such topics. She argued that academe is covertly still recreating rather than evolving as this illustrates that the same patriarchal academic culture is still valued. Because publication is valued for promotion and tenure, she concluded that women may be tempering their work to gain entry in the top-tier journals to get tenure. As a result, Hart noted such feminist voices are still silenced within the academic culture. Clark and Corcoran (1986) hypothesized that women are judged by an inner circle of accomplished male professors who may assess their social entrance into the profession negatively rather than assessing their work and academic accomplishments. Using such avenues to keep women and academics of color at bay is a subtle but destructive form of aggression. Lane (2005) reported that male faculty in particular have no idea how their behavior affects women and the academic work climate.

Fairweather (quoted in "Market forces," n.d.) suggested how institutions will be distinctive in the marketplace, that is, by how they respond to changing demographics. As institutions increasingly move to more corporate ideals, the need also arises for more part-time and nontenure-track professionals. Historically women and minorities have filled these positions. The move to reduce tenure stream positions, historically held by males, for cost-savings purposes has a corporate grounding. These changes increase dissonance and inequity (Glazer-Raymo, 1999). Thus begins the story of the second and related precipitating force: the introduction of the corporate culture into academe.

7

Corporate Culture in Academe as a Precipitating Circumstance

I just look out the window and see what's visible—but not yet seen.

Peter Drucker

Faculty members have no recourse but to circle the wagons, to accept a labor-management relationship.
James Duderstadt and Farris Womack

Academic Culture as Henhouse

Academics are not only supposed to govern the means of production; they are the means of production. They self-govern. They are the hens; and theoretically they govern the henhouse. They own the eggs, and they let the kindly farmer know how many eggs they are going to lay, if any, over a given period of time. Even if the hens are capable of laying one to two eggs in twenty-four hours, they decide how many eggs they want to lay, where in the henhouse they would like to lay them, and even if they plan to lay any eggs at all. Thus, normative poultry standards are set by the self-governing hens, not the farmer.

The farmer accepts and supports their decision and agrees to provide them with the henhouse, straw, roosters, feed, and water to allow them to facilitate egg production however they choose. The farmer is never sure how many eggs there will be to sell or if the hens are going to provide the eggs to sell once they lay them.

The farmer cannot be sure if they will be Grade A extra-large eggs, double-yolked eggs, or small eggs. Why the farmer is happy with this arrangement is not known, but the hens are happy, and that is all that matters to the hens and the farmer, because theoretically and philosophically, happy hens produce when their needs are met.

Suppose the kindly farmer retires and is replaced by a new henhouse administrator who is not happy with the current arrangement or with the previously hen-established poultry standard. The new administrator shifts the focus of egg production to a more corporate model and emphasizes the bottom line. The new tagline is: "More eggs, more profit. Better eggs, happy customers." Somewhere in there the hens should be mentioned, but they are not.

These bottom-line concepts work better in places where the owner of the company also owns the means of production. Although the henhouse administrator cannot lay the eggs and thus has no control over their number, size, or quality, he or she wishes to regain control of the hens and the henhouse, setting new terms and imposing new standards. Forget that hens know eggs and egg production better than the administrator does. Hens know nothing about the bottom line, marketing, distribution, or customer satisfaction.

When the hens are informed after the decision is made and imposed on them, they are very unhappy. The new henhouse administrator insists that he or she now controls the hens, and pushes for greater production. The hens will still receive the henhouse, straw, roosters, feed, and water, but the quality and quantity will be linked with their ability to produce according to the new poultry standard set by the henhouse administrator. There is no guarantee that the hens will get the desired location for their nest, the softest straw, the tastiest feed, free range, or be awakened by the most melodious of crowing roosters. In addition, the henhouse administrator intends to use tactics to make the hens feel guilty and inadequate if their production level falls below two eggs per twenty-four-hour period so as to affect the bottom line positively. In other words, the new henhouse administrator seeks to enforce a poultry standard that may not have been agreed on by the hens. Furthermore, the administrator does not really care what the hens think.

According to the new administrator, if the hens do not produce the requisite daily quota, they may find themselves the juicy centerpiece in a bowl of chicken noodle soup. In this case, regardless of who owns the means of production or thinks he or she does, the new henhouse administrator is still at the mercy of the hens and their power to control egg laying in order to fulfill his or her dream of large-scale egg production and success in the egg market. But the hens are pressured to affect the bottom line, which they had never been forced to do before. And, frankly, they do not care about market share. All they really care about is free range, soft straw, virile roosters, tasty and plentiful feed, and cool water. The eggs then follow naturally and systematically. To attempt to change this process, that is, to step up production, goes against nature and what hens have been deciding and doing for centuries.

To anticipate what the hens will do now under the pressure is anyone's guess. Perhaps they will be too stressed to lay two extra large Grade AA eggs every day. Perhaps they will be too stressed to eat or drink properly to achieve a contented state, which will affect their egg production and quality. Perhaps they will turn on each other or the rooster or even the henhouse administrator as a result of the added stress. Some may choose to sell the eggs they produce to a third party and feather their nests.

By the same token, within the university, no matter how corporate and business-like the administration wants to become, the faculty will always own the means of production. The university is knowledge driven, and faculty possess the knowledge. Universities, in shifting their focus to a more corporate mentality, have inadvertently or conveniently forgotten their most important asset: the knowledge producers, be they faculty or professional staff. Although there is no way to know if these changes in academe will create additional workplace or henhouse aggression and incivility born of resistance, we believe that greater awareness of aggression will force workplaces like academe to examine themselves and address these formerly ingrained, tolerated, and rewarded practices. This chapter examines the corporate culture being imposed on the traditional academic culture and its effect.

The Emerging Corporate Culture

Winston (1997) argued that colleges and business have definite similarities. However, because colleges are nonprofit but still sell a product or service for a price, they function differently than a business does. Corporate culture has its own set of values and practices entrenched in bureaucratic ideals and management strategies that are somewhat foreign to academe (Abdennur, 2000; Weber, 1948). Pricing strategies like tuition discounting coupled with buzzwords like *excellence* and *quality* offer strange paradoxes to higher education (Winston, 1999). Readings (1996) argued that the university's role as purveyor, reproducer, and proprietor of culture, knowledge, and cultural capital has been gradually replaced by a corporate push for quality and excellence. Higher education has switched ideologies from concentrating on what is taught to students to producing excellence. Excellence is not a thing but a qualifier. It is a corporate term adapted to nonprofit higher education that replaces traditional academic ideals. Previous sharing of and building on academic ideas, cooperating with colleagues on scholarship, and team teaching have given way to market philosophies that emphasize competition, capturing market share, and taking sole proprietorship of intellectual property, all in the quest for excellence (Hoel, Faragher, & Cooper, 2004; Powers, 2003; Washburn, 2005).

Braskamp and Wergin (1998) advocated that the original motive for cooperation and scholarship was to promote the commonweal. With the ascendance of the corporate culture, some faculties have come to realize that their position can be used not to promote the common good but to enhance their own social and cultural capital, which has political implications. Corporate good does not always align with public good. Oddly, this is what is implied, if not set out explicitly, in university mission statements and guiding principles. Corporate culture is a new concept to some faculty and one that is difficult to reconcile with their expectations for teaching, research, and service. Therefore, the value of a faculty member may largely be determined by his or her contributions to the field or discipline in terms of articles, books, presentations, and grants, for which tenure, promotion, and merit pay are the rewards. The process is viewed as an exchange. Entrepreneurial faculty say that altruism has been supplanted by personal monetary rewards, but not to the exclusion of tenure and promotion (Zemsky, Wegner, & Massy, 2005).

Faculty research interests that spur knowledge development are as unique as the faculty researcher. Under a corporate cloud, however, knowledge generation tends to develop along fiscal lines favoring topics that are likely to attract grants, business and industry funding, and individual prestige (Gould, 2003; Helgesen, 1997; Slaughter, Archerd, & Campbell, 2004; Washburn, 2005). Knowledge for knowledge's sake is replaced by knowledge for exchange (Gould, 2003). What faculty teach will be needed and valued as long as it has exchange value for students seeking majors that result in well-paying jobs. Knowledge will become mitigated by outside entities rather than be controlled by universities, as was traditionally the case.

The contentiousness toward one another at faculty meetings was in the context of a more general upheaval in the whole college—new president, old dean left, a general sense of strife, angst almost—that seemed to set everyone on edge. If you examine where we were going, it was tied to resources, and some departments fared better than others and a lot of contention around political battles. There were always factions. The people were holding onto their fiefdoms come hell or high water. A graduate program at an extension campus was closed. . . . The department was under real duress. It was not doing well financially. The department was not mentioned in the dean's strategic plan. — Caroline

When issues come up, no one in the department is ever going to vote any differently than how this bully wants them to vote. The VP may make changes when he restructures, but nothing has been done yet. The program director and his sidekick have brought in a lot of students and run on-site programs so the administration is reluctant to do much because money [from tuition] is involved. — Ben

---

Finally, knowledge will be packaged in consumer-friendly, attractive, digestible, affordable units (online or watered-down modules, for example) as determined by consumers rather than by faculty. In a corporate culture, this is necessary to affect profit margins and pushes for excellence. Gould (2003) said that the introduction of corporate ways would shift "learning as a competitive right" to "learning as a purchasable commodity" (p. 72).

I guess budgets are tight all over, but the dean's push for market share is driving many of us crazy. We keep hearing about preserving the mission and striving for quality and excellence. But then we hear that if we don't start offering online courses to increase revenue in the college, some other nearby institution will. So which is it, mission or market? I thought we as a faculty would discuss alternative approaches to increasing enrollment, but it seems that decision was already made for us. We are forced to go in the direction management wants to take us when we can't reconcile it to what is best for our program. — Abby

According to an interview given by Fairweather ("*Market forces*," n.d.), competitiveness increases as prestige increases. However, lower-status institutions seeking to compete against higher-status institutions feel they must imitate the higher-status institutions to succeed. Everyone is struggling to compete for students and copying or imitating what they perceive others are doing successfully. Shifting academic values to market values affects how faculty react. When rewards are tied to the shift, administrators are under pressure to perform. They push faculty to make changes that in some cases affect autonomy and academic freedom in order to address bottom-line economics. Faculty tensions mount, and role ambiguity rises (Washburn, 2005).

I don't know if it is all the pressure we are under to get things done at an appropriate time. . . . The pressure of the job makes people uncivil, and more is done under the table, and you are discriminated against in other ways. — Lucille

The increased degree of external research and the pressures that places on higher education has situated academe in a vulnerable and precarious position. This is especially critical because it invites mission creep. Morphew and Hartley (2006) conducted a document analysis of missions of four-year institutions to determine if what the institutions say about themselves aligns with their institutional type as determined through the Carnegie Classification. They may not, because mission statements have become tangential to marketing and recruitment efforts and strategic planning. Consequently, the university mission statement is focused less on what the institution is and more on what it needs to be to attract and retain the kinds of students and faculty it wants. However, chasing market shares and ignoring mission in the process will hurt the university more than the money will probably help it (Zemsky, Wegner, & Massy, 2005).

Historical Background on the Corporate Culture

Vannevar Bush regarded universities as the logical place to do research because they are unencumbered by the profit motives of business and industry and because they promise support, security, and intellectual freedom. However, what seemed like a giant leap forward for university research function was not without consequences (Zemsky, Wegner, & Massy, 2005). University research ultimately spawned economic development, research parks, and think tanks and created consumerism, commercial product development, and business and industry partnerships. Twenty-five years ago, Baldridge (1971) acknowledged that the university was undergoing massive change; however, comprehending and enduring the momentum of market forces was overwhelming to faculty.

Faculty's limited political sphere of influence was tested. The political struggle began with the social conditions that promoted and supported special interest groups and their concomitant values. Eventually the interest groups pressured for change. Baldridge (1971) acknowledged that the changed and often fragmented collegiate structure became vulnerable. The sense of power and autonomy of the faculty was impinged on. In fact, in the latter part of the twentieth century, it was encroached on by the Total Quality Management (TQM) and Continuous Quality Improvement (CQI) movements (Deming, 1986). Still, faculty did not see their work as businesslike or the students as customers (Horine, Hailey, & Rubach, 1993). Isolated pockets of TQM/CQI threatened faculty and traditional academic values (Keashly & Jagatic, 2003).

Since the early 1990s, however, the new consumer approach has manifested itself in competitive market strategies and taglines designed to attract students to campus (Bowen, 2001). Market forces have clearly driven student choice of academic major over the past few decades. There have been decreasing numbers of humanities and social science majors and more professional and semiprofessional career majors (Zemsky, Wegner, & Massy, 2005). However, because market forces dominate, faculty have been forced to alter their values because students are buying more seats in the professions and fewer in the humanities and social sciences.

Change and Shifting Ideologies

To support the notion that higher education is embracing a corporate model, Rossides (2004) remarked that colleges and universities engage in tuition raising much as businesses engage in price wars. Market forces, managerial accountability, budget strategies, student as consumer, and university as knowledge seller signal major shifts in academic ideology (Duderstadt & Womack, 2003; Hoel & Salin, 2003; Shelley, 2004). These real as well as ideological changes from a reactive, nonprofit academic focus to a money-conscious, proactive, market force have spawned faculty reaction (Hood, 1994). It has not been positive: competition has ignited discontent, skepticism, cynicism, resistance, suspicion, and bitterness with the possibility for self-destructive behaviors that would serve to increase divisiveness (Murphy, 1999).

While these ideological shifts may legitimize behaviors as necessary to accomplish newly stated goals, they are uncommon elements in traditional academic culture. Autonomous work that faculty did previously may be displaced for greater control of work by administrators. This shifts the collegial culture to a managerial one, forcing a once-dormant negotiating culture to grow in response (Bergquist, 1992). Faculty shift their efforts away from a traditional academic value system to address managerial and administrative directives whether they want to or not. Administrators shift academic priorities in accordance with market quality and trends, often without including faculty. Faculty are nevertheless expected to comply with the administrative directives regardless of their effect on rigor. Work norms become less clearly defined, and feelings of disenfranchisement arise. Faculty may resort to political strategies in order to negotiate with administration as a means to try to preserve traditional collegial norms. They may become passive-aggressive and slow to change. Tenured faculty may resort to micropolitics to preserve their eroding territory, power, and control, and untenured faculty may be victimized because they are naive and unprotected compared to senior faculty (Hoel & Salin, 2003).

As has been the case with other industries, market-driven objectives will likely transform the academic culture and environment into a corporate entity despite faculty strongholds on traditional academic norms and values. Rosenzweig (1998) and Duderstadt and Womack (2003) have noted that consumer and corporate rhetoric have entered education in other ways, through online programs, corporate training colleges, and e-learning for nontraditional students. Promoting the virtual university and attempting to remake the face-to-face, on-campus university more virtual in order to compete for market share supports a movement toward a corporate culture. Duderstadt and Womack noted a tendency for institutions to bundle services, market degree programs as customized to fit student needs, and mass-produce a course so that it can be marketed globally. As a result, faculty are forced to modify their instructional delivery to accommodate student desires because the corporate culture emphasizes customer satisfaction (Readings, 1996).

Corporate Culture and Academic Norms and Values

Administrative leadership styles have also taken on a corporate tone. A shift to corporate norms allows the market to control the institution rather than presume the faculty will continue to govern the university. Duderstadt and Womack (2003) noted that "faculty members have no recourse but to circle the wagons, to accept a labor-management relationship" (p. 96). They advocate that the more a college education is seen as a personal marketable commodity and less as a commodity to improve the public good, the essential academic values so strongly upheld in traditional education will gradually erode in order to harbor more interest in private sectors. The tug-of-war inherent in the transition from the traditional academic to the corporate culture will increase the instances and degree of workplace aggression just as it has in industry.

When I worked outside academe, I dealt with people and the bureaucracy, but the university is different. My male colleague explained that with faculty, it is very personal. In the bureaucracy, my role and my position met someone else's role and position in the bureaucracy. My higher ed colleagues were attacking me as a person, and the only way I could fight back was to attack them personally. [My colleague] said I was too nice a person to do that. . . . You can separate the person from the position when you have tenure, when you have academic freedom. — Caroline

---

Zemsky, Wegner, and Massy (2005) and Washburn (2005) also discussed the shift from mission-driven organizations to market-driven ones and the consequences of that shift. The trade-off to accumulate more market share, that is, more students, and income means an imposition that causes the university to divert the money earned in larger programs to offset costs in smaller departments that serve the mission. This shift toward a market share mentality favors more profitable programs. This ultimately forces less profitable programs out of the academy and their faculty as well—but not without a fight.

Managerial Culture and the Corporate Model

Universities are becoming more managerial and strategic, espousing visions, and responding to satisfying consumers' and other stake-holders' wants and needs (Lewis & Rayner, 2003). This change usually causes faculty frustration because forcing these changes are devoid of proper rewards and incentives. The lack of support to assist faculty when administration responds to these market forces exacerbates the aggression that typically arises (Owen & Demb, 2004; Twale & Lane, 2006). In other words, if the administration expects more from faculty such that faculty autonomy is weakened, then accountability on the part of faculty should also be lessened and subsequently assumed by the administration.

While Senge (1990) regarded tension as necessary for growth, change, and creativity of the organization, economic tension seems to raise competition in the faculty. For instance, increasing reliance on part-time faculty, adjuncts, and nontenure-track instructors' positions widens the gap between tenure-track and nontenure-track faculty (Zemsky, Wegner, & Massy, 2005). This corporate move is a sign of faculty devaluation and unbundling of the professoriat. This results in turf protection (in the curriculum, for example), plots to outwit administrators, and retreats into disciplinary silos. Some faculty still work for the university, while others act more like self-employed subcontractors working at the expense of the university and bettering themselves.

Corporate Culture and Institutional Mission Shifts

Links between these faculty and administrative tensions, aggressive behavior, and shifts in the managerial cultural normative expectations may also stem from changes in the academic culture brought on by institutional changes in the Carnegie Classification. The desire to change university mission and vision to something new, address new groups of clientele, and reward new work behaviors in response to the shift in classification may have contributed to greater faculty aggression and incivility and greater administrative tolerance of it. Changing university classification at any institution to increase the research function means increased expectations for success of faculty by administrators. For faculty, this change often means unrealistic goals for increased research production and less time for teaching, which was heretofore recognized and rewarded. Clashes between faculty and administration could fuel workplace aggression toward colleagues and administrators.

For instance, faculty at seven community colleges regarded the mission statement and the actions of their employing institutions as inconsistent with one another (Levin, 2006) such that "disagreement between faculty and administration on the decision-making process is evident" (p. 79). Levin concluded from his extensive interviews and focus groups that "faculty are compromised" (p. 84) now because faculty work is economically defined by the institution, but faculty values of teaching, service, and advising are not. Faculty values are more philosophically and morally defined, but administrations forced to be more corporate in nature may be trying to redefine those staunch values as economic, and that is exacerbating the tension. This represents a significant change in value orientation for faculty. While the faculty express tension in this values conflict, they do not openly oppose it. Perhaps some of the tension is more latently than manifestly resolved. In a corporate culture, what the administration values is not always what faculty, especially old guard faculty, value. Unfortunately, should one part of the existing culture wish to change something staunchly held by the other part, a period of "domination and resistance" usually ensues (Eagleton, 2000, p. 123). Political maneuvering takes over such that the culture can harbor an active struggle or ignore one that rages beneath the surface. Those who ignore the struggle insulate themselves from it in their self-imposed silo. Others may choose to bully others to regain the old values.

Evidence of Corporate Culture and Entrepreneurialism in Academe

The introduction of corporate cultural values into a traditional academic culture shifts alignment because old values no longer interconnect with new management practices (Smart & St. John, 1996). These practices eventually determine where resources are allocated and who and what is rewarded and valued in academe (Schein, 1992).

My mentor and another male faculty member blocked my contract renewal. What went on there was groupthink, and no one was going to go against that male faculty member. I appealed. The appeals committee bypassed the dean and provost and sent it directly to the president, but he went with the faculty. Because we did not appear in the strategic plan, he may not have wanted to put any resources into the department. — Caroline

---

Faculty can see the academic culture move to assimilate a corporate culture philosophy and value system and struggle with the alignment of the language of learning with a strange language of commerce. Reflexively, faculty resist and recoil at the thought of a corporate organizational structure because studies of business and industry management have found bullying, incivility, and camouflaged aggression present (Gould, 2003; Hoel, Faragher, & Cooper, 2004; Hoel & Salin, 2003; Lewis, 2004; McCarthy & Mayhew, 2004). These same things begin to surface more in academe.

To improve customer service and increase recruitment and retention, academic and nonacademic areas compete for money in order to exist, subsist, and persist. Zemsky, Wegner, and Massy (2005) labeled this "administrative entrepreneurialism." Their goal was to function in the black, not in the red. Previous guardians of the educational gate shifted their focus to become guardians of the till. This spurred the campus bifurcation between the academic and nonacademic camps. Faculty argue that education is a privilege for students at the postsecondary level and a competitive one at that (Gould, 2003). Under those circumstances, faculty who own the means to production, that is, knowledge, determine as experts and creators of knowledge what is to be disseminated and to whom. Faculty, as part of a university governance structure, control the curriculum and the grade. They bring stability and represent the intellectual capital, that is, the brain trust of the institution. Now, that role has been supplanted by "best-buy" lists in popular magazines that have fueled greater need for university branding, strategic planning, and alternative budgeting plans that favor profitable departments producing higher student outputs over those that do not (Gould, 2003). Mission-driven philosophies determining placement in the pecking order have been replaced by profit margin philosophies that harbor competition and increase threats of extinction for lower-producing departments. It is difficult to implement communities of learning and encourage communities of scholars under such circumstances. In fact, some faculty members have discovered that through the corporate culture, they can benefit personally by becoming entrepreneurial rather than teaching and researching to benefit the greater good. Internalizing the values of a corporate culture by faculty also has the potential to change the altruistic nature of knowledge development and dissemination.

Washburn (2005) provided evidence that faculty and administration "desire to maximize their own entrepreneurial returns from academic knowledge" (p. 70). Administrator emphasis on research versus teaching under the new corporate model requires balance; however, unexplained imposition by administration on faculty has caused tension. Faculty haggle over intellectual property issues and wage legal battles against the university to determine ownership of that intellectual property. One could argue that the freedom of faculty intellect and scholarship has created controversy over intellectual property rights. For instance, university research done for the public good has spurred competition, patent rights, and technology transfer to outside companies or faculty-based businesses (Slaughter, Archerd, & Campbell, 2004).

As a result of the move to greater consumerism in higher education, universities have become less the watchdog of public interests and more the lapdog of private interests (Washburn, 2005). Reconciling this change has caused faculty to sway from a community of scholars tradition and reconfigure itself as a community of competitors struggling for scarce resources. Bland, Center, Finstad, Risbey, and Staples (2006) raised the following query: "What impact are institutional-level changes in faculty role having on morale, collegiality, and respect within departments, faculties, and institutions" (p. 118)?

The Rise of a Culture of Incivility

With the emerging corporate culture in academe, we draw on game theory to explain a rise of incivility and a bully culture. Barash (2003) argued that humans have natural inclinations to pursue self-interests that may not be in the best interest of the whole group. In academe, for instance, each faculty member, especially those who are untenured and on the tenure track, is trying to maximize his or her skills. To do this, they collaborate to maximize those interests through coauthored articles, grants, conference proposals, and symposiums. This is what is expected as normative collegial, academic behavior. However, introducing market forces into academe might increase the tendency for faculty to work alone and compete for those scarcer resources instead of working together to maximize work output and organization goals simultaneously. Barash indicated that this rests on how faculty view their work, as either mission or market driven, which colors the inclination to be cooperative or entrepreneurial. Less choice in a particular field usually shifts the focus to personal rather than social causes (Lindholm, 2004). A faculty member weighs personal values with potential benefits to determine which approach works for him or her. A faculty member who chooses the entrepreneurial route may do so with the understanding that he or she is more likely to help than hurt the university. Using game theory, this logic works if only a few people become entrepreneurial. However, with prosperity likely as a result of following market forces, other faculty will follow when they see the benefits that accrue to colleagues who have preceded them in these ventures. This increases competition and tension among faculty. Members of the group who do not jump on the bandwagon may resent what some colleagues are doing, considering it not to be in the best interest of the university. They also see that in most cases, the academic culture supports or does not discourage this new entrepreneurial spirit. While the market-driven university pushes the entrepreneurial group to succeed, the mission-driven faction attempts to rein in those it regards as double dippers (Barash, 2003). In either instance, it pits faculty again faculty and ideology against ideology. The likelihood for uncivil action and bullying increases.

What is likely to happen in this situation is that any negative behaviors go unnoticed because the academic culture absorbs, buries, sanitizes, or excuses profitable entrepreneurial behaviors (Barash, 2003). A monkey-see, monkey-do mentality begins when faculty realize the benefits of moving in another direction. The largest payoffs seem to go to the entrepreneurs who take advantage of the autonomy and academic freedom given to faculty, that is, they maximize autonomy and academic freedom to their own benefit. It probably seems to the mission followers, however, that while they are upholding the university ideals, their academic freedom and autonomy are being eroded as the administration caters to the entrepreneurs.

At the same time, faculty who choose not to take advantage of the situation can easily develop resentment toward those who do take advantage of the opportunity to make money. In the long run, regardless of how much one is entrepreneurial to the exclusion of the mission, the whole enterprise will suffer. The entrepreneurs eventually lose a personal stake or interest in the university. Barash (2003) contends that when faculty members feel isolated, they are more likely to follow market opportunities than support the mission. If administrators and faculty are focusing on the bottom line and market share, they may be overlooking, ignoring, or sidestepping destructive behaviors that are occurring directly in front of them (Bennis, 1989; Campbell, 2000).

Zemsky, Wegner, and Massy (2005) remind us that "the university remains a sanctuary apart from the hurly-burly of the marketplace" (p. 69). Unfortunately, the university values entrepreneurialism for its own benefit to the university coffers and image. Faculty may be competing for prestige, status, and value on campus while making greater income off campus (Barash, 2003; Newman, Couturier, & Scurry, 2004; Zemsky, Wegner, & Massy, 2005). Campuses compete for top faculty, and faculty do what is needed to be competitive among colleagues. Administrators and faculty may suspect that entrepreneurial colleagues may boost the reputation of a departmental faculty, but inside the department, tension between egos and resentment rises.

Bland et al. (2006) argue that paradigm shifts in appointment type to accommodate corporate shifts in philosophy constitute an unbundling of the faculty role and expectations that differentiate faculty status. This perhaps has implications for how one group of faculty interacts with others informally and formally. In their study of full-time faculty, Bland et al. found that the rationale for tenure versus nontenure appointments had less to do with strategic planning and more to do with autonomous, isolated subunit decision making. These types of tactics pit faculty against administrators who encourage this type of hiring as cost-saving measures. These management directives deviate from expected and traditional academic behaviors (see also Schein, 1992). The result is cognitive dissonance, which has proven repeatedly to be a fertile ground for bullying, camouflaged aggression, and mobbing (Gayle, Bhoendradatt, & White, 2003; Peyton, 2003; Rayner, Hoel, & Cooper, 2002; Sheehan & Jordan, 2003).

Part III

Addressing Faculty Incivility and the Academic Bully Culture

All of the pieces in the adapted Salin (2003) conceptual framework have been assembled in the previous chapters. In this final part, when the motivating, enabling, and precipitating factors come together as Salin indicated, the chance for incivility and the bully culture to take residence in the workplace will be greater than if these forces are not present together. With the enabling and motivating structures and processes in place and the impact of precipitating forces, workplace harassment and camouflaged aggression continue to rise. A case has been made that an academic bully culture has formed and flourishes in the university. Suggestions for addressing the bully culture and the culture of silence that surrounds it and alleviating the anxiety associated with victimization follow in Chapters Eight and Nine. They contain helpful information and suggestions for dealing with bullying in the academic workplace.

8

Characterizing the Bully Culture

For wherever there is jealousy and selfish ambition,
there you will find disorder and every kind of evil.

James 3:16, New Living Translation

Faculty recognize that tenure offers relatively secure employment. Some may presume they can do anything they please. Left unchecked, however, any aggressive behavior not reprimanded may escalate into increasingly more serious behaviors. With the specialization of academic disciplines and professions and the rise of the corporate culture, faculty members may inadvertently dismiss aggressive behaviors as typical of the times or treat them as a trade-off for the personal autonomy they enjoy. In actuality, an academic bully culture may be functioning due to prevailing assumptions, newly adopted corporate values, and unwitting personnel. In time, such behaviors become accepted as necessary to accomplish tasks or perhaps for senior faculty to increase their power or move up the administrative ladder. Bully behaviors become institutionalized within the culture, strengthen it negatively, and are transmitted to the next generation of faculty. Faculty may not recognize existing leverage that will help alter a bully or mob culture.

Warning Signals

Barometric pressure in an organization may be measured through astute faculty and administrative recognition of prevailing problems. These problems manifest themselves through typical workplace warning signals. If not addressed, these warning signs become characteristic of the academic culture and organizational structure. Their presence can precipitate conflict and increase anxiety. Warning signs of incivility and further disintegration to a deeply ingrained bully culture begin with low morale, high turnover, increased early retirement, and increased absenteeism and tardiness; diminished work quality of once-productive people; new faculty struggling to survive; increased illness and health issues; working at home more than usual; lower or poorer work quality; increasing faculty isolation and alienation; a low degree of meaningful faculty participation in governance activities; poor faculty performance patterns illustrated through low research productivity and poor teaching evaluations; and consistency of poorer faculty performance evaluations (Davenport, Schwartz, & Elliott, 1999). In addition, Kezar (2000) found that misunderstood, disrespected, and disenfranchised faculty and administrators exit universities, most often citing conflict and miscommunication. Some are concerned as to what has been contained in their personnel files that may not be reflective of their work.

With all the funny business going on, I requested to see my personnel file. The HR guy went into a state of panic and stalled me. After I returned from leave, I asked the HR guy for my folder again, and he said he would ask the VP if I could see my file. I wanted to see what was in there. — Ben

---

What could logically be the result of academic bullying tends to fall under what Huston, Norman, and Ambrose (2007) labeled *disengagement.* They found in their research that productive senior faculty experience a negative, often traumatic experience in their department or college and subsequently disengage from collegial discussions, campus service, department socials, and junior faculty mentoring. Instead already productive faculty channel that negativity into positive other-focused activities that improve their teaching and enlarge their publication records, and often they engage in professional service off campus and pursue consulting opportunities. They also found that a typical faculty response among the disengaged manifested itself in exiting the institution, withdrawal from it, silence or its opposite (speaking out against injustice), or cynicism and sabotage. Bully cultures can emerge within the cultures of silence and cynicism and set in motion long-term consequences for the institution.

Warning signals may be telling, if and when they are noticed (Montez, Wolverton, & Gmelch, 2002; Rosser, Johnsrud, & Heck, 2003). However one major reason that these warning signals may go unnoticed is that recognizing workplace aggression and doing something about it are not part of the standard graduate curriculum or the socialization or professionalization process of junior faculty (Weidman, Twale, & Stein, 2001). No one is really sure what he or she is looking for. Furthermore, attempting to deal with workplace aggression within the university organizational structure often dwarfs the person or victim seeking justice or restitution. When unsuccessful, the do-gooder often experiences powerlessness or helplessness (Dziech & Weiner, 1990).

A faculty colleague who left had an exit interview with the provost and mentioned things that were going on in her department, and to my knowledge nothing was ever done to change them. — Lucille

---

Faculty and administration need to ask themselves the following questions:

- Where are the pressure points within my smaller department and the larger organization?

- Is morale low? Why?

- Is turnover high? Why?

- What are the work patterns over time?

- What is the tenor at faculty meetings?

- How would one describe faculty demeanor toward one another? Are colleagues uncivil to one another?

- Are there opportunities or committees where individuals can bully others and remain undetected?

- Are there situations that harbor bullying yet have been ignored?

- Does the organizational tolerance for bullying create mutual acceptance for such behaviors?

- Is bullying a learned behavior supported in the culture and the organizational structure, and do certain organizational structures attract bullies?

Perceived Backlash of Existing Sexual Harassment Policy

Within academe, it is possible that the presence of sexual harassment policies that define inappropriate behavioral expectations of a sexual nature have overshadowed more subtle forms of workplace harassment. In an overzealousness to address and confine sexual harassment, we may be overlooking a broader problem of workplace harassment that begins with uncivil acts that come to include camouflaged aggression, passive aggression, bullying, and mobbing. Passively, supervisors may be uniformly misinterpreting or failing to acknowledge that when harassment is not of a sexual nature, it is still harassment and must be addressed (Rayner, Hoel, & Cooper, 2002). The presence of sexual harassment policies may be inadvertently forcing other aggressive workplace or camouflaged behaviors to continue because only sexual behaviors, not those general behaviors, are included in many existing documents. If no policy exists to address anything other than sexual comments and behavior, then types of aggressive behaviors may by default be deemed acceptable (Rayner, Hoel, & Cooper, 2002).

When universities formulated and adopted policies on the more obvious acts of sexual harassment, they overlooked that the acts may have been symptomatic of a generally uncivil environment. However, the presence of sexual harassment policies and the concomitant sanctions offered to eradicate that problem provided campuses with a false sense of accomplishment for two reasons. First, the underlying problems that caused sexual harassment may also fuel general workplace harassment. However, only one area of harassment was subjected to identification and sanction, and general workplace harassment was overlooked. Perhaps because many victims were female, the aggressive actions were all lumped under a sexual harassment umbrella. Second, harassment of a sexual nature is unacceptable, and by default then, other forms of harassment may be acceptable because they were not included in the stated policy. So long as perpetrators did not step into the realm of sanctioned sexual harassment, their actions were permitted to continue in academe. Fueled by precipitating forces, an academic bully culture is born and nurtured by inattention (Brodsky, 1976; Dziech & Weiner, 1990; Rayner, Hoel, & Cooper, 2002; Richards & Daley, 2003).

Initially, to address all types of workplace aggression, existing harassment policies, which may include only unacceptable acts of a sexual nature, should be reevaluated and recalibrated to be more inclusive (Rayner, Hoel, & Cooper, 2002; Richards & Daley, 2003). Richards and Daley caution, however, that policies that focus only on individual acts of bullying will not eradicate an entrenched mob or bully culture. Depending on how entrenched this culture is, eradication could take years or decades. The immediate passage of sexual harassment policies did not contain sexual harassment. Despite university policies, procedures, and sanctions for sexual harassment, there is no way to know how many instances are not reported formally. Kelley and Parsons (2000) found that the longer one's tenure at the university, the number of times one was harassed increased. This indicated to them that policy did not necessarily curtail the problem.

Often faculty members became repeat victims because they did not pursue redress through formal channels. A reason for not formally filing a complaint was the belief that if the perpetrator were harshly dealt with, then the victim would also undergo a thorough investigation. Because the victim knew she would have to work with or encounter the perpetrator in the future in the institution, there was a desire to stop the harassment but not risk maligning relationships or risk further harassment. Kelley and Parsons (2000) concluded that perhaps less harsh sanctions might have encouraged victims to come forward and file a complaint.

The research by Kelley and Parsons (2000) presented an interesting caveat to the call for policy: policy may not be valuable because sexual harassment policy was less effective than originally planned. Campuses might first do assessments on the effectiveness of their existing policies and revise them accordingly. The absence of reported action may not be because of a decline in the problem but rather the fear of exposing the act and, more important, the perpetrator and the victim.

Stopping Victimization

Getting involved in identifying the bully, stopping the victimization, or changing the culture has little precedent or immediate reward in academe. The perception is that there is risk without guarantee of gain. Dziech and Weiner (1990) suggested that any incivility problem should not be denied or attributed to another explanation. Incivility should be treated as such. It is important to identify the uncivil behaviors and the bullies performing them and avoid passing their actions off as academic freedom, autonomy, shared governance, idiosyncrasies, or ego.

Creamer (2004) advocated that academic environments that successfully manage conflict through valuing openness, civility, and honest communication are more likely to survive. Casbon and Hurtig-Casbon (2005) also described healthy, nonviolent organizational environments as open, fair, and balanced. Sheehan and Jordan (2003) addressed ways to train people to curtail bullying, incivility, and aggression by exposing it. Once it is exposed, it can be dealt with openly and systematically. To accomplish this, victims need to make a risk assessment in terms of the degree of harm caused by the bully, along with the extent of support they will need once the act is made public (Hoel, Faragher, & Cooper, 2004). Victims will be more likely to act if support exceeds risk. Eradicating a culture of fear is imperative in dealing with bullying. However, Richards and Daley (2003) caution that this is only one victory, not the whole war. Salin (2003) indicated that it is difficult to keep the enabling structures, motivating processes, and precipitating forces from coming together to form a bully culture.

Awareness and Sensitization

In higher education, we acknowledge the presence of or potential for uncivil behavior among students through the establishment of student codes of conduct (Peck, 2002). Most, if not all, campuses have a student code of conduct. Has anyone stumbled over a faculty code of conduct anywhere? Probably not. Faculty disciplines and professional areas have codes of ethics that relate only to how research should be conducted and disseminated. Campuses also have policies, procedures, and committees for the proper conduct of research involving human subjects. Actions outside research and publication are unlikely to be formally regulated. Academics are highly educated people, hardly the sort who need policing, and that may be why there is no formal faculty code of behavior.

Yet a faculty code of conduct sounds like a good idea. Would faculty be interested in formulating such a code for themselves? Would they read such a policy if one existed? And would they follow it? For centuries, society has relied on higher education to produce gentlemen, ladies, good citizens, moral beings, and principled leaders. With new groups on campus and the introduction of the corporate culture as possible reasons for increased incivility, faculty seem to act more on individualistic interests and less for the common good. In fact, they act less like good academic citizens and more like independent contractors. Thus, faculty self-interests may unwittingly foster incivility (Peck, 2002). With no code of behavior (and we are not recommending one), the chances for greater incivility have the potential to fuel the bully culture. However, if faculty remain silent and continue to dance around the issue, they need to be cognizant of what is going on in academic culture.

Schlossberg (1974) noted the influence of institutional barriers, glass ceilings, and the "internalized social attitudes and norms" that limit people's progress upward (p. 262). Over thirty years ago, she called for those on the bottom of the hierarchy to challenge the elite at the top, knowing an "era of distrust" would likely result (p. 262). She predicted that if challenged, administrators would claim that fairness and equity had been employed and women (and minorities) would be able to produce evidence of inequality. For women to challenge administration openly would mean raising administrator anger. In a culture of fear, this is unlikely. However, Schlossberg recommended role reversal, so that minority groups, women, and administration could experience the life of the others and see each other's perspective as a starting point for dialogue (Mead, 1934). Until we experience life from another's perspective, even if it is a sensitization exercise, we really have no idea how victimized people feel and how they respond. And if bullies do not recognize they are bullies, they can never change their behavior.

Faculty and staff need to be educated about uncivil behavior, its context, and its consequences to the workforce and how it evolves into a bully culture (Davenport, Schwartz, & Elliott, 1999). Graduate and professional programs do not ordinarily teach the need for civil behavior toward colleagues as part of a formal or informal curriculum. Therefore, educating junior and senior faculty on the matter appears necessary so that they can pass it along to the next generation of faculty. Faculty can learn civil behavior in the same way they learn uncivil behavior (Bandura, 1973). Why not entice faculty to be civil by providing opportunities to indulge and practice civility rather than incivility?

Campus committees are a place to begin, especially considering the politics and power wielding that may be taking place on them. The communication process may appear to be civil, but in reality the outcome may be calculated and downright uncivil. Campuses have sensitivity training for violators of sexual harassment policies, and perhaps the uncivil committee members need a similarly devised sensitivity training program that is broader and asexual in nature. It may be wise in the interest of awareness for all administrators and faculty to attend such a workshop separate from sensitivity training for violators. In fact, Hannabus (1998) recommended offering conflict management for perpetrators and assertiveness training for victims of bullying. Katz (2006) also recommended instituting or reinstituting some standards of acceptable behavior that address faculty professional obligations. He added that professionals who practice more self-reflection regarding their professional behavior and their responsibility to others would serve themselves, their colleagues, and the university well. This might be addressed in an awareness workshop.

Socialization and Education

Montagu (1956) contended that "man is tailored according to the prevailing cultural pattern into which he is born" (p. 58). Just as culture and society help us learn civil behavior through example, observation, and reinforcement so too can incivility be learned and perpetuated if reinforced (Peck, 2002). Peck's position begs the following question: Is there any faculty training for academic civility, or is it assumed and predetermined? Just as we seldom emphasize formal pedagogical training in graduate school or through professional development in many disciplinary areas, we do not emphasize formal training in civility either. We assume it was learned earlier (in kindergarten, perhaps). With this in mind, how we socialize graduate students and new faculty into a department affects how they act toward colleagues and others. If they enter an uncivil culture, they are likely to exhibit behaviors that are uncivil or be treated uncivilly themselves. Damrosch (1995) indicated that in order to address concerns of how faculty acts, we might restructure graduate work and include ways to teach and socialize novices to be civil academics and model what that entails. He called for a balance between an intellectual tendency to isolate, or exile ourselves, and the need to collaborate more with others.

Nevertheless, we may be unaware when incivility arises. For instance, in graduate school, a doctoral committee chair who is arrogant and self-centered but significantly published in his or her field or able to attract large grants could get away with acts of incivility. Published works and grant money have high totem or exchange value in academe, and universities are reluctant to challenge the behavior of such totem holders or academic stars. Therefore, their incivilities may often be explained away as idiosyncrasy or eccentric behavior. Some students will be repulsed by these uncivil behaviors, but others, focusing on being stars themselves, might see it as expected, as academic survival, as nature-of-the-beast behavior, and perhaps accept arrogance and incivility as normal. They may practice similar behavior in graduate school or later in their careers. In other words, faculty may be unobtrusively modeling uncivil acts, and graduate students may be inculcating uncivil behavior without realizing it is happening. Uncivil faculty may be passing their incivility along to subsequent generations of new faculty, thereby perpetuating the bully culture (Bandura, 1973).

Not everyone participates in uncivil acts. However, there is the possibility that an uncivil environment has allowed bullying and mobbing to flourish. If it happens once without sanction, it will likely happen again (Bandura, 1973). Bandura offered hope through the same theoretical premise: if we can learn incivility, we can unlearn it and relearn civility. This area begs for more research as to how graduate students and new faculty are socialized and how the learning and relearning processes take place. Do these groups that enter as outsiders initially see incivility taking place? Newcomers are in the best position to notice it. What has been their observation as to how it is handled? Do they see reason to adopt such behaviors to succeed?

What Peck (2002) called the "incivility spiral" may have been exacerbated by the increased use of the Internet and e-mail, impersonal forms of communication. With these technological advances, acceptable communication behavior changed. Peck acknowledged that civility cannot be completely present in a society or organization, and so some incivility is expected and absorbed without repercussions. Finding out where one's academic culture and climate falls in relation to civility and incivility is helpful in pinpointing problems. Faculty and departments should take note of their communications to one another. In retrospect, are more communications to colleagues done more impersonally than personally?

Are they impolite or polite? Are they a result of technology, overwork, alienation, time constraints, efficiency, corporate values, or dislike of colleagues? Do colleagues give timely responses or curt dismissals? Do communication patterns support a bully culture?

Gamson (1997) and Tierney (1997) called for greater social relearning to counter the trend toward fragmentation and individualism in academe. Tierney said to be clear as to what is expected of faculty in order to manipulate the culture to reward for desired change. This would suggest revisions in the socialization process to socialize for the desired outcomes by providing novices with clear performance guidelines and expectations. Better definitions of and expectations for teaching, research, and service are necessary at faculty hiring. Exposure to these guidelines in graduate school is also recommended. People acting on their own individual expectations rather than on commonly agreed on, clearly articulated norms could be averted. Without that knowledge, actions are based on perceptions, which may really be misperceptions and might lead to negative behaviors.

Second, Tierney (1997) encouraged a more fluid, flexible system to accommodate change and new ideas and voices. He also suggested behavior modification of sorts rather than rewarding poor behavior. He claimed that in order to foster a learning organization, faculty should do a better job of inculcating civil behaviors and monitoring their own behavior, pointing out unacceptable behaviors when they happen rather than turning a blind eye. In other words, this approach is preferred to formal policy that calls for an administrator to use sanctions. Relying on administration to interpret and administer policy uniformly is precarious. Faculty members need to be aware of their own uncivil behavior first, correct it, and not passively sit by and tolerate colleagues' being uncivil. Bennett (1998) referred to this "culture of shared responsibility" as one that needs incentives to encourage faculty cooperation. This requires working together to develop those incentives, tangible and intangible.

Whether graduate student or junior faculty, novices need to be attentive to problems, details, committee procedures, and actions taken on their behalf. New entrants would do well to learn about their department, school, and university culture and prevailing climate and read the policies and the formal documents that govern them. This is especially important for junior faculty on the tenure track. These groups need to be students of higher education: they must observe, listen, gather artifacts, ask questions to learn how the structure functions and governs itself, and determine who has the power in the organization and who has the authority. They must be active learners of the academic culture and climate at both the macro and micro levels; read higher education texts and articles on the professoriat and how it is changing and what the concomitant repercussions are; assume the role of anthropologist and study the culture as a participant observer or ethnographer; and understand why things happen, happen slowly, or never seem to happen at all. To read and analyze the culture is to be savvy to the absence of expected behaviors and the presence of unexpected behaviors. They can consider taking some courses that focus on postsecondary education. Campuses might offer a certificate program in higher education or, at the very least, periodic workshops to facilitate the learning of academic culture. Cultural anthropologists, organizational sociologists, and social psychologists would have a great deal to contribute to these sessions.

Sheehan and Jordan (2003) believe that a true learning organization would potentially minimize incivility and bullying. Bullying would likely exist in organizations where those with the power tolerate and reward bully behavior, either consciously or unassumingly. Determining this requires examining the organizational power relationships and power distributions within an organizational structure. These may be sources of the problem.

To foster a learning organization, graduate programs need to include workplace aggression, bullying, and mobbing awareness as part of the program. Topics can be addressed in law, sociology, business, and education classes that focus on legal issues—specifically, what the organization's or employer's responsibility is to the employees and what recourse battered employees have. Graduate counseling programs could feature these topics in their courses from the victim's treatment perspective. Leadership programs would focus on recognizing and acknowledging uncivil behavior and preventing and remedying workplace harassment through organizational change and policy formulation courses. Sociology and anthropology courses could examine aspects of the bully culture (Sheehan & Jordan, 2003). Political science programs could cover the politics associated with bullying.

Leadership and Education for Change

Bennis (1989) argued that someone will need to come forward and lead academe out of its troubles, preferably somebody whose words are not simply rhetoric but rather someone who understands leadership for change. To be enamored with one's own words and plans devoid of honesty and real substance and action would overlook the opportunity to propose solutions to the problems, modify behavior, or readdress the mission. Owen and Demb (2004) noted also that addressing the gap in functional ways through leadership intervention was necessary to reduce tension and uncertainty.

To understand and make meaning from campus situations, Bensimon (1990) suggested that educational leaders take time to decode people's actions and campus events because each has symbolic meaning that contributes to the larger picture. She reminded us to note what aspects of culture uphold or support these meanings and what aspects are challenged and who is doing the sustaining and who is challenging the status quo. Considering the symbolic meaning and implications of actions and artifacts is essential for holistic understanding. Decoding the symbolism is imperative to understanding what is really going on.

Although I go out of my way to teach and advise students, my attitude toward the institution has changed. I don't feel as loyal to the institution. When asked to contribute to the capital campaign, I said the reason why I am not giving is because I have been blacklisted from the grad courses. I was willing to give 10 percent of what I earned in those courses but no courses, no 10 percent. Feel free to tell the president. There is some of what the institution will lose — not the students, but the institution. I also go out of my way to avoid being on a committee. — Ben

Kezar (2000) noted that misunderstood, disrespected, and dis-enfranchised faculty and administrators exit universities citing conflict and miscommunication, among other things. Kezar also found that where one sits in the organization affects one's perspective on leadership and how it functions or malfunctions. Faculty who see themselves as empowered lead and act quite differently from faculty who view their relative positioning as servants to the administration.

In the meantime, I do my job. I work well with the other profs in my department. I am trying to make inroads into another department and at other institutions. In general it is a pleasant place to work. But I make statements as the conscience of the group. I don't try to anger anyone. There isn't too much you can do. You get passive. You can't make yourself sick over it. — Ben

Leaders must be tuned into their department, school, or college or university rather than outwardly focused or simply ego centered. Ignoring problems, covering them up, passing them on to subordinates and replacements, or losing them through the committee process does not solve the problems. Such inaction spawns more problems. When they show leadership for change, administrators and faculty act as social architects (Bennis, 1989). These architects for positive change must be known and respected in the academic culture before they can effect change or resolution, as the culture will dictate who, how, and what is needed and tolerated. Bullying and aggression in the university are conflict like any other, a challenge indeed and an opportunity to be resolved, not repressed (Bennis, 1989).

Social architects can be servant leaders. These people would be in a position to deal with incivility and bully cultures in ways that autocratic or laissez-faire style leaders could not do as effectively. Servant leaders are empathic listeners who push for openness, greater awareness, and persuasion. They do not need to be in administrative positions to lead. They often see the bigger picture beyond the bounds of time in order to envision change that will occur in the academic culture and the organizational structure as a result of change processes. Servant leaders affect the whole community, not just warring factions within. Their goal is to solve problems and not bolt, leaving a mess for the next leader to discover and resolve (Spears, 1994).

Power and Academic Citizenship

Ideologically and practically, not every faculty member in a department holds the same view of academic citizenship. Differing views, and especially those that deviate from the prevailing normative expectations, cause opposition. These normative standards advocate that to be a good citizen, faculty should perform integrative citizenship (Parsons & Platt, 1970) through service opportunities, peer review, accreditation self-study, program evaluation, and curricular revision. Academic citizenship becomes difficult when department faculty do not share the same departmental goals or share them but differ on how they should be reached. In fact, disciplines like psychology, sociology, history, and English have splintered as a result of multiple perspectives. Paulsen and Feldman (1995) cautioned that one group has the power to marginalize another, thereby disrupting or thwarting integrative academic citizenship.

Greenleaf (1970) contended that "most of us are more coerced than we know [and] we need to be more alert in order to know" (p. 33). Part of the socialization process is to ascertain who in the academic environment possesses the power and who has the authority. Both can be vested in the same person, but in many instances, the person with the power has no authority and the person with authority is accorded little power by others. Who has power? How much? What kind? How is it wielded, toward whom, and how often (French & Raven, 1960)? Who has authority, what kind, and how is it used (Weber, 1948)?

Faculty need to address their autonomy and academic freedom and how these sacred tenets might be enhanced or diminished by powerful colleagues and masterful administrators. Knowing what effect corporate culture strategies are having on the professoriat is important:

- How does administration treat change? Is change imposed on or shared with faculty?

- How is the administration addressing the imposition of the corporate culture?

- Are administrators overly concerned with customer service, quality, and excellence?

- Are tenure-track positions diminishing in exchange for greater cost effectiveness?

- Do administrators who control budgets speak of capturing market share?

- Does administration include faculty in strategic planning?

- Do faculty feel that individual autonomy is eroded as a result? Do programs designed to capture market share compromise academic freedom or autonomy?

- Do faculty feel less power to control the changes?

- In the midst of all this, on whom are faculty members and administrators taking out their frustrations?

Kezar (2005) noted the need for equalizing power because the collegial model implies consensus. By contrast, hierarchical power implies managerial strategies. She cautioned that before we adopt corporate models and philosophies we must consider the problems likely to emerge. Although it may be too late, she added that perhaps the adoption of radical change is not worth the resulting problems. She suggested that if we make changes in governance, we must also align cultural values with the changes. Faculty need to be included in the process. This raises additional questions:

- How are our academic values aligned with our actions?

- Do we abandon our academic values for market share?

- Can we strike a balance?

- How does corporate culture change academic culture?

- What adverse actions can be expected from such a change?

Not only do faculty have power; certain documents and committees that purport shared governance possess great power (Rayner, Hoel, & Cooper, 2002). For instance the promotion and tenure document and committee are perhaps the most powerful in academe because they validate faculty careers. Statements in promotion and tenure documents guide the early careers of junior faculty. Tenured and promoted members appointed or elected to that committee control the future rank and status of candidates. Imagine the dynamics of that committee if key players use their power to bully prospective candidates or faculty members on the committee by breaching confidentiality or unjustifiably posturing for or against a candidate. The same dynamics may be found on faculty search committees or graduate admissions committees (Giebel, 2005). Budget committees or administrators in charge of budgets have the ability to nurture or starve a program or individual. Similar opportunities exist for faculty during end-of-the-year performance evaluations when power vested in supervisors allows them to withhold merit increases unfairly or without substantial explanation (Peyton, 2003). To acknowledge the power and authority differential is to begin to redefine and redistribute power with an aim to neutralizing a bully and a bully culture. Patience and data-based research are needed to exhume all of the myriad skeletons buried in academic closets.

9

Challenging the Academic Bully Culture

*Behold the turtle. He makes progress only when his
neck is out.*

James Bryant Conant

Data Gathering and Analysis

Knowing the number of instances that bullying has been reported
and policy responses to those bully behaviors is a way to determine
how widespread and entrenched bullying and mobbing are in
the workplace. Faculty and administrators may want to study
incivility, bullying, and mobbing on macro and micro levels. On
the micro level, we recommend first examining the extent and
types of policies written on workplace harassment as a separate
entity from sexual harassment. Do workplace harassment policies
even exist? If they do, on what areas do they focus? Is the policy
fairly comprehensive? On a macro level, we recommend noting
how many academic institutions have sexual harassment policies
compared to how many do or do not have workplace harassment
policies. The number of policies to address incivility has increased
(Peck, 2002) but not uniformly (Twale & Lane, 2006). Dziech
and Weiner (1990) recommended that harassment complaints be
handled by support staff, for example, by starting a confidential
hotline. This also serves as a data-gathering opportunity to find out
how widespread workplace harassment is in academe and where
it is located. Making it confidential increases the likelihood that
victims will respond.

Action Research

Because each department may be different, we recommend research on a smaller scale using action research principles. In terms of addressing an academic bully culture, departments, schools, and colleges and universities need to know how faculty work together, how the culture and climate relate, and how the organizational structure factors into the mix (Cornesky & McCool, 1994). Action research can also be used to chronicle change and how the department handles it. In addition, what effect has change had on the culture and the faculty? How do faculty react to change? Who instituted the change?

Yoder (1985) recommended action research approaches as a means to fix one area at a time rather than conducting national studies. She also encouraged program evaluation as a way to unearth underlying problems or trends. Due to the variations as to how bullying manifests itself and how victims react, it makes sense to study the problem case by case. A comparison of many cases over time may lead to the development of a comprehensive or uniform policy stance.

Other Research Techniques

Beyond, we encourage gathering longitudinal data on campus turnover, absenteeism, health issues, office hour patterns, productivity levels, committee assignments, committee meetings attended, and committee decisions rendered. We recommend chronicling the number of aggressive instances reported and responses made to uncivil behaviors that exist in an institution (Ferris, 2004; Jennifer, Cowie, & Ananiadou, 2003; Peyton, 2003). These data can be used to determine patterns that have formed over the years. For instance, over time, faculty in a department or college may keep fewer and fewer office hours, which could be attributed to increased levels of individual versus collaborative productivity. Or the data may show something different: a decrease in office hours and a decrease in research productivity could indicate the existence of a bully culture.

Discourse Analysis

We encourage discourse analysis of workplace harassment policies. Specifically, we suggest that faculty and administration look at the intent and extent of policies. If this means first examining other policy documents that govern faculty work, we encourage a careful examination of the spirit of the documents, how they are worded, how they are interpreted or misinterpreted, how often they are examined, and how they are used, among others.

Cultural Audit and Consultation

More systemic approaches to addressing incivility in academe are needed. Consultation with experts in the areas of bully behavior and academic culture is suggested to determine the extent of workplace aggression. We recommend beginning with a cultural audit from an outside consultant, which might be helpful as a means to shed light on and improve an ingrained academic bully culture.

In a culture audit using action research techniques, it would also be helpful if faculty chronicled their perceptions of their academic culture—their goals as well as the perceived barriers to those goals—and how colleagues regard each other and are supportive of others' goals (Aquirre, 2000).

Asking faculty to match the organization chart to the inner workings of the cogs and wheels in the organizational structure would also be valuable. These questions could be posed (Aquirre, 2000):

- What are the standards of behavior in a department?

- How do people get along? Over what do they argue? On what do they agree?

- Is the department cliquish?

- What are office hour patterns?

- Are the faculty social?

- Do faculty seem disengaged?

- Do they support or criticize administration?

- How does the academic culture respond to change? The threat of change? The inclusion of different groups?

- How does the culture respond to new market forces and consumer demands?

- How does each gender and ethnic group view the other groups socially, politically, academically, and collegially?

- What do the culture and the organizational structure do separately and in tandem to construct barriers to promote inclusion or exclusion?

- What do the culture and the organizational structure do separately and in tandem to construct barriers to permit incivility and bullying?

- How do the culture and organization share the negotiated social identities of women and minority groups in academe? In other words, how do minority individuals cope, adjust, reconfigure, and adapt?

- How do majority groups react to the efforts of the nonmajority?

After assessing the overall environment ask the following questions:

- Do we have reason to believe that incivility is a learned behavior supported in the culture and the organizational structure?

- Do the bully and the institutional tolerance for bullying create mutual acceptance for such behaviors?

- Is there dysfunction in the department that draws bully personalities to the job?

- Do bully personalities stay because the prevailing environment tolerates and often inadvertently rewards their behavior?

- Do bullies profess to support the organization goals by whatever means it takes, including bullying?

- Do bullies create a supportive bully culture?

- Does the culture create the bully as a survival tactic?

- Are bullies justified using survival tactics because their supervisors are also bullies?

Archival Data

Neilson, Pasternak, and Van Nuys (2005) offered a conceptual model of organizational types that illustrate nonfunctional or dysfunctional environments that subsequently allow the organization to malfunction. Elements of these environments can be used as a barometer to identify negative situations and behaviors within an institution. Departments need to look historically at how they have functioned—or malfunctioned, as the case may be. Gathering archival data can be helpful to detect trends. It will answer questions such as these:

- What are the turnover rates?

- What is the proportion of tenure and promotion appointments to attempts?

- How long do chairs and deans serve?

- What do exit data show as to why faculty leave the institution?

In addition, merit raises and salary compression patterns could also be very enlightening.

Stemming from research by Twale and Shannon (1996) regarding the nature of service, women were more likely than men to seek service opportunities outside their departments. Participating in the department is likely to place women under greater scrutiny, and therefore women tend to seek opportunities external to campus to fulfill service obligations. To gather data on this, begin with these questions:

- Do majority colleagues include minority colleagues in decision making and social events? Who mentors them?

- Do male and female colleagues include each other in collaborative fashion or as outsiders?

- Who mentors whom? Who goes to whom for advice?

- Where do women and minorities seek to fulfill their service functions?

- Where and on what types of committees do women gravitate? Do women and men share in the campus governance process in terms of numbers as well in positions and on all types of committees?

- Do women and men share equally in professional service in terms of numbers, positions, and functions in local, state, regional, national, and international organizations?

- If there appears to be a gender imbalance, what data help explain it?

Data Analysis

The result of the data gathering should produce a bully barometer of sorts (Jennifer, Cowie, & Ananiadou, 2003). It should indicate if there are problems and from where they might be coming. The result might lead to these questions:

- Are there indications of tension but few reports of harassment and aggressive behavior?

- Are there indications of fight more so than flight, self-preservation, and denial (Ferris, 2004; McCarthy & Mayhew, 2004; Peyton, 2003; Smith et al., 2003)?

- Are there reports but no policy on how to resolve issues? This challenge makes addressing the issue a priority and can be accomplished by first examining policies to see if the problem is or has been addressed.

- What kind of reaction does a specific work environment support? If there is policy, the victims may be more prone to stay and fight. If not, then flight and denial are more logical responses.

Faculty, Administration, and Policy Direction

If workplace harassment flies under the radar of existing sexual harassment policy, then a harassment policy needs to identify additional types of aggressive situations through the sanction, dismissal, or demotion of perpetrators. Participants in our sample for the most part had no recollection whether their institutions had any workplace harassment policies. At least one institution did, but the faculty knew nothing about the policy. It is one thing to formulate policy; it is another to acquaint faculty and administrators with its existence on a regular basis. Policies need to be enforced and monitored. The success of policy formulation will ultimately be determined, however, by the sanctions imposed and the ability to reinforce those sanctions, and information we compile from an assessment of the outcomes.

Academe poses another conundrum. Tenured faculty who bully cannot be terminated as easily as administrators. That gives us hope that administrators who bully can be terminated as administrators. Unfortunately, the administrator who bullies will simply return to a faculty position and likely find opportunities to continue being an aggressor (Ferris, 2004).

Peyton (2003) suggests that if bullying is permitted to prevail in the culture, it must have been created and supported by the managers and administrators overseeing the organization. This is a bold accusation. Rayner, Hoel, and Cooper (2002) contend that if a culture harbors bullying behavior, a change in culture can diminish or eliminate these aggressive, dysfunctional behaviors. Perhaps that begins with an examination of the administration and its role in a dysfunctional culture. Is it upholding policy or resistant to policy formulation on bullying? Rosenzweig (1998) noted that "change produces stress, stress provokes divisions, and divisions require acceptable arrangements for resolution" (p. 117). However, those who have spent decades in academe realize change and resolution are easier said than done. Are there institutional and cultural means to purge academe of incivility, mobs, and bullies? Does it begin with the administration?

Formulate Policy

All institutions should formulate a workplace harassment policy if none exists. If it does exist, then it should be revisited periodically, with new data in hand, to determine if it needs to be revised. Policies already in existence may need to be amended to include a broader range of harassment issues (Hoel, Einarsen, & Cooper, 2003). Policy will be more effective if the root cause of the incivility, bullying, and workplace aggression is determined first. It begins with identifying the imperfections in the organizational structure and culture and then determining what the structure and culture and the administration do to address incivility and bullying from a policy perspective. The process ends with a plan that can be implemented to alleviate such behavior and identify how the policy will be disseminated.

Rutgers dean Barbara Lee (2004), coauthor of the most comprehensive and widely used higher education law text, stressed the importance of clear policies and guidelines in faculty handbooks. In an interview, she asked if the campus faculty handbook specifically stated expectations for civil behavior from faculty, staff, and the administration. If it does not, she asked how we can assume that people faced with myriad problems, circumstances, and limited resources can always be civil. If we cannot assume civility all the time and have reason to believe that the prevailing academic culture tolerates incivility, then, she asked, how are uncivil behaviors treated and sanctioned? Lee followed with inquiry into whether the sanctions that have been written have been followed and tested. These questions suggest that faculty and administrators examine their faculty handbooks searching for references to workplace harassment in its broadest sense. Campus dialogue in faculty senates and faculty forums, data gathering, and the need to write collaboratively any policy to address it can be undertaken by institutions in ways that are relevant and appropriate to each campus.

Strict policies put into place should force management to stop any aggressive behaviors. If your institution does have a workplace harassment policy, what is covered in it and what is not compared to other policies in existence? Note also what types of behaviors have been addressed on campus through discipline and grievance committees as an indicator of prevailing cultural norms. It is wise to examine the track record for the filing of, disposition of, and sanctions from sexual harassment policy violation cases. If the record shows that many have been filed but few have reached resolution and sanction, then it speaks to the possibility that workplace harassment policies probably do not exist, and if they do, they may not be followed. Is there a relationship between the lack of resolution in sexual harassment cases and the absence of workplace harassment policy? Specific unacceptable behaviors may be present in various types of sexual or workplace harassment policies but not all behaviors are covered by policy. Bullying can continue in an organization where there is no existing policy or little or no adherence to existing policy (McCarthy & Mayhew, 2004). Sexual harassment policy may be perceived to cover all problems. Its existence gives license to some bullies and mobs to justify their behavior as not violating a particular policy because what they did was not sexual in nature. They cannot be charged with more general types of workplace harassment if there is no policy for it (Rayner, Hoel, & Cooper, 2002).

Establish Grievance Procedures, Sanctions, and Redress

When we have to use policy to control uncivil or bully behavior, we have moved away from social control through informal folkways and mores governing faculty behavior (Peck, 2002) to a more formal enforcement. This is an indication that faculty are not policing their own behavior and therefore must rely on external policy and sanction to police themselves.

Grievance Procedures

Concomitant with policy formulation is the examination of campus grievance procedures that may or may not yet address issues related to harassment in the workplace (Westhues, 2005). While workplace harassment policy may be formulated, does the campus grievance procedure document parallel language in the workplace harassment document? What is the relationship between sexual harassment policy and workplace harassment policy and grievance procedures? Are administrators, faculty, and grievance committee members familiar with workplace harassment and the policy covering it?

First, faculty need to determine if existing grievance committees have the jurisdiction to hear cases regarding workplace harassment. Once it is determined that they have that capacity, the committee response is perhaps as effective as the extent of an already established bully culture. For instance, grievance committees to which bully and mobbing victims would seek redress may encounter a committee making recommendations to central administration. These committees could act as conduits or smokescreens that administrators use to legitimize their final disposition or decision in grievance cases. If administrators overrule committee recommendations, they diminish the spirit and power of the committee. To establish an environment that values honesty and civility, overturning decisions needs to be considered carefully and explained accordingly given that some committees may be acting as mobs, knowingly or unknowingly.

Using internal grievance procedures may not protect the victim as much as it protects the employer-administrator of any liability (Namie & Namie, 2003). Similarly, Franke (2005) found that workplace policies rarely include retaliatory acts or language dealing with such actions. To find links between initial actions and retaliatory reaction is difficult, but careful documentation by victims often bears out the complaint. Policy may need to be changed to address the handling of acts of retaliation as separate from initial acts of workplace aggression.

Sanctions

Informal control through mores and taboos allows a group to police itself. Law and policy are the last resorts to changing behavior because they are imposed from the outside. Part of that dictates that administrators must now enforce the imposed sanctions (Davenport, Schwartz, & Elliott, 1999). We struggle with the notion that some punishment is better than none because of the symbolic message it sends. However, a lighter sanction may send the same message as no sanction, that is, workplace harassment is normative, and somewhat acceptable, because response to it is not harsh. And punishment for the perpetrator could help to bring closure for the victim, regardless of how severe it is. To reiterate, however, harsh sanctions may deter victims from identifying bullies for fear of more retaliation.

Redress

It is difficult, though not impossible, to overcome the personal, psychological, and professional damage and losses resulting from bullying or mobbing. Furthermore, without clear policy that stipulates redress beyond sanction, redress is tenuous. Most of the victims would be happy with a public flogging of the perpetrator or a complete overhaul of their department, school, or university, but that is not likely. Tenured perpetrators are difficult to unseat as faculty, although they can be asked to step down as administrators. If there is no policy in place or no clear enforcement of existing policy, the problem may lay dormant, to reappear later. Campuses with harassment policies in place may ask perpetrators to attend sensitization seminars, curtail their activity on committees, or procure a formal apology to the victim.

Perhaps the best form of redress comes from public disclosure of the bullying so everyone realizes who the perpetrator is and what intolerable acts have been done to the victim. The campus administration must realize that it is not too late to formulate policy so bullying does stop. Formal redress may be an area ripe for legal intervention such that given sufficient documentation, victims can take perpetrators to court in much the same way that sexual harassment cases have been resolved. Publicity generated from these cases is sufficient reason for campus administrators to take action to prevent bullying and mobbing.

Deconstruct to Reconstruct

Social learning theory works both ways: we unlearn and then relearn to produce a desired result (Bandura, 1973). Unrewarding uncivil behaviors and rewarding civil behaviors is a simple solution. Just as cultures can nurture aggression and aggressive people, relearning can reduce aggressive levels (Bandura, 1973). If, for instance, faculty act in certain ways to secure tangible rewards, then the reward structure can be altered to secure the desired behavioral outcomes. Aversive consequences are one means to accomplish desired behavioral outcomes using a peer approach rather than a one-on-one tactic. For instance, what is the department rewarding? Who is being rewarded? Is the department, committee, or administration rewarding behaviors toward a desired communal outcome, or is it rewarding behavior that facilitates someone's personal agenda?

Faculty in an entrenched academic bully culture may have a vested interest in sustaining a mob mentality at the expense of identifying and eradicating one token bully (Bandura, 1973). The bully can be ousted, but the toxic culture still remains. It appears that defusing of the bully scores a victory, but it may be short-lived if a silent mob still reigns to strike another day. Punishment therefore needs to have a collective quality as well as a superordinate-to-subordinate, one-on-one feature so that the solution is more systemic than localized. Social change is possible if the culture reinforces the punishment through aversive means as a way to encourage mobs to reregulate and disavow old bully tactics. One bully may be easier to rehabilitate, whereas a mob backed by a bully culture is a greater challenge (Westhues, 2005). Rehabilitation of the bully requires close supervision to see if behavior modification is working. Goals set for the bully need to be achieved. However, trying to eradicate the mob and modifying a bully culture is more difficult using an approach that merely covers up but does not correct.

Changing behavior is much easier, however, than changing values, attitudes, and beliefs ingrained in faculty and in their culture. Therefore, systemic modification would best be monitored from someone outside that academic culture. Faculty would be held to a higher accountability standard for their individual actions rather than perhaps being allowed to camouflage them in committee decisions, for instance. External administrative hiring would be preferable to internal promotions as a means of introducing new blood and new expectations for behavior into the system. It may send the message that a bully culture has been identified and its actions are under scrutiny. Those externally hired need to be change agents with no vested interest in preserving a dysfunctional culture. This is easier said than done because bullies and mobs will take out their frustration on these new employees.

While change is happening around us, we as faculty may be less inclined to discuss the implications of adjustment as a means to prepare ourselves to address the issues. We may be more inclined to retreat to and react from silos or isolated pockets. Because faculty members are competing for scarce resources, they have become more isolated, disconnected, and entrepreneurial and less collaborative than they perhaps once were. Some faculty members have chosen to champion their own self-interests rather than those of the institution. Mallard (2002) called faculty who, in the search for scarce resources, exhibit jealousy and isolation "fiercely independent." If faculty use camouflaged aggression to secure scarce resources, it may go undetected (Abdennur, 2000; Hoel, Einarsen, & Cooper, 2003). In fact, it may be explained as culturally acceptable (Rayner, Hoel, & Cooper, 2002).

Abramson (1975) mentioned faculty dual citizenship, that is, as part of the problem and part of the solution. Faculty participate in pluralistic decision making through committees and also practice peer review. The latter has the potential to breed mediocrity as much as it does elitism; neither is healthy. Without clear-cut guidelines or training for unbiased decision making and peer reviewing, both administrative and peer actions can be arbitrary and self-serving, accompanied by little or no accountability to others. The absence of effective leadership breeds tolerance of the mediocrity or elitism that leads to dysfunctional environments.

Strategies for the Victims

Bullying acts and mob behavior are inconsistent with the normative expectations of a civil society regardless of what an academic culture has come to define as normative. Some faculty and administrators are dreaming of and romanticizing about what wonderful academic departments and organizations they have, often oblivious to the stark reality that they preside over dysfunctional departments and may be responsible for harboring and nurturing dysfunctional cultures. In other words, victims of workplace harassment see the same department and organization differently from others.

Well, one doesn't ever really expect [incivility], particularly from colleagues and administrators. Mostly I feel that the incivility was unfair and misplaced. . . . I can't say I understand much of it. I try to not reciprocate, and as a rule I do not confront people unless they are inhibiting my action. Otherwise I get a little pissed off and hold it until I get home. . . . If I think that I am being treated unfairly, I say so and then let it go (or I try to let it go). — George

---

As a result, bullies and mobs need to realize how far adrift their actions have become (seemingly on behalf of the organization) in order to help themselves relearn and self-regulate (Bandura, 1973). This is assuming they are not engaging in such behaviors knowingly and willingly, in which case they would have no desire to change. However, under the guise of academic freedom, autonomy, and shared governance, faculty and faculty committees could camouflage bully behaviors and underlying motives such that a bully's personal maneuverings emerge as sanitized, collectively reported committee decisions (Abdennur, 2000; Lewis, 2004). In other words, it is business as usual.

Be Assertive

Individuals who are bullied and allow themselves to be bullied continually need to be more assertive and to learn to control aspects of their current condition (Bandura, 1973). This implies that victims of bullying and mobbing may have the answers in their cultural toolbox already but fail to see these answers. In addition, as academics, faculty presumably have the training to problem-solve logically, but those faced with being bullied may not be able to garner the resources needed to stop their own victimization. Faculty can be led by the bully, or they can maintain integrity, exercise power, and oppose the bully or mob. Victims must recognize they have power too and take the risk to exercise it rather than ignore, isolate, or seek jobs elsewhere—activities that simply reinforce the bully. Of course, this is much easier than done.

[Being bullied] made me angry, and I have always stood up to the bullies because I know that their qualifications and experiences are weaker than mine. That is why they are bullies. A strong professional is a threat. — Janice

---

One way to deal with bullies is to challenge them and not cower or back down (Namie & Namie, 2003). Klein (2005) learned from experience that being banished to the fringes at the hands of a department tyrant forced him to decline service opportunities at the behest of his bullying colleague. On the most positive side, the mob inadvertently freed the time for him to develop an impressive list of scholarly contributions to his field. Success, in this instance, can be the best revenge. Giebel (2005) analogized his plight to Daniel in the lion's den: he was entertainment for the unfulfilled spectators. His remedy for others who have been harassed and bullied is to speak out. "Daniel" need not be the food that feeds the paranoia that causes victims (and witnesses) to remain silent. He tired of being the victim. Klein's power was ultimately manifested through his scholarship, which has totem or exchange value in the academic marketplace.

According to Davenport, Schwartz, and Elliott (1999) the victims of bullying and mobbing have choices. They can develop coping mechanisms that help them survive in their existing environment. Some escape physically to another job, and others, like Klein (2005), escape mentally to better opportunities in the position they already hold. Some brave hearts choose to gather information and eventually blow the whistle on a bully, and some seek legal redress. Those with a strong vested interest will champion policy development if no policy exists. Perhaps all victims, regardless of how they manifest the challenge, will find ways to build their self-image and restore their self-esteem.

Seek Information and Resources

Several sources provide additional help and information. It may prove advantageous to locate helpful Web sites that post information on workplace aggression, incivility, bullying, and mobbing, as well as offer general direction for redress, sanction, and grievance procedures. Some may be general or institution specific. The *Chronicle of Higher Education* periodically carries stories of faculty who have been victimized in the workplace. Counseling and mediation services are recommended for faculty and administrators who are not only victims but also perpetrators. We recommend that bully victims begin the dialogue within a campus's local chapter of the American Association of University Professors.

Those who have been victimized by bullies and mobs need not be reminded to document everything. Victims already know to do that. Documenting the obvious is one thing. However, this type of detective work requires a certain level of assertiveness because it must be performed under a cloud of perceived defeat. Colleagues and administrators who support a bully culture probably dismiss victims. These people may also have more enticing goals to fulfill than to be mindful that one of their colleagues is being victimized.

Garner Power

According to Namie and Namie (2003) and Miller (1986), cautiously and methodically airing the problem is recommended over a period of time. Immediate gut reaction to confront the bully or mob publicly as a means to resolve the situation is not recommended. Victims should avoid or curtail contact with the bully or his or her allies and correct the situation in the best way possible, avoiding knee-jerk reactions that are generally more reactive than proactive and often done without forethought (Goffman, 1967, 1974). A poorly thought out reaction or response may be too little or too much as it relates to the infraction. We suggest the biding of time be used for a strategy of gathering data by listening, observing, documenting, and engaging other colleagues in casual conversation. Colleagues unknowingly may be sources of information even though they are not bullies or part of a mob. You will likely find out that some colleagues are complicit in the bullying or mobbing acts.

Departments are small worlds, and colleagues may have seen and heard something without realizing its significance. Our data-gathering and cultural audit thoughts suggest doing an ethnography. This data-gathering process is no different from one used by any trained qualitative investigator. The suggestion is to be your own advocate and do your own detective work. It may be the best offense a victim has.

Typically faculty members with doctorates have written a dissertation. Earlier we said victims have power, and here is a chance to use it. Apply the investigative and analytical skills used in the dissertation and subsequent research studies to this dilemma. Like all other good research, the best approach is to pause and put the disparate pieces of information together before acting.

Victims have the power to unobtrusively collect their data in the guise of their own academic freedom and autonomy (Klein, 2005). This requires the victim to document what is not always obvious. The obvious statistics reflect department, college, division, or university trends. The data that victims gather are more person and situation specific. We suggest victims not only note what is visible but also take account of body language. Who is allying with whom? What are the stakes or rewards to be gained by bullies or mobs? How are people acting toward you? How does it differ from before the uncivil or bully incident? How are people acting toward your closest colleagues? Has victimization by association begun to occur?

We also suggest that once victims gather all their data, they analyze and share this information with a close friend or valued colleague. According to Goffman (1959, 1963), it may be necessary to interpret the information in context. We do not imply that someone else must validate the claim of victimization but rather to ensure that all data have been gathered and analyzed to a reasonable conclusion, just as in an action research project. The relationship can affirm the direction to take with regard to the data gathered. Once the data are reviewed, then some action may need to be taken on behalf of the victim, whether it is to inform an administrator or confront the bully or mob. If there is a need to confront the bully or mob to fulfill legal protocol, the victim should be prepared to do that (Klein, 2005; Westhues, 2005). Confrontation should be written rather than verbal in order to support the paper trail. Some states honor conversations documented through hidden tape recorders, and others do not. Klein noted that victims need to be prepared for anything and everything. Most of all, victims owe it to themselves to not be labeled as victims anymore.

Epilogue

We have presented the pieces of the conceptual framework of Salin's research (2003) and illustrated them through faculty experiences. And we have offered suggestions for dealing with incivility, workplace harassment, camouflaged aggression, bullying, and mobbing. We have now reached the end of the book but not the end of the story.

If indeed academe has become more uncivil, how do we rebuild it to be civil once again, assuming from Chapter Two that it ever was civil? If faculty have the ability to transform higher education for a new generation, its hallmark need not be a continued legacy of incivility harbored by its organizational structure and academic culture (Finkelstein, Seal, & Schuster, 1998). Unfortunately, we are less self-governed and ruled by internal moral codes of ethics than we are ruled by more external pressures and formulated policies. Thus, our challenge lies ahead.

Acknowledgment that there is a problem is the first step. Are workplace bullying and faculty incivility born of resistance to outside pressures? Are they simply indicative of academic culture? We believe that greater awareness of academic culture, organizational governance structure, corporate influence, and multiple perspectives has implications for exposing workplace aggression, faculty incivility, bullying, and mobbing. These behaviors will force academe to examine itself, its faculty, and its policies and address any formerly tolerated practices. We leave you with more questions in hopes that you will extend the conceptual framework and the conversation with your colleagues:

- Has anything that you read in this book resonated with you? Are you a victim or a perpetrator?

- Will anything you have read in this book cause you to examine your institution's workplace harassment policy?

- Will anything you have read in this book make you more cognizant of whether your performance on university or college committees promotes bullying?

- As you read this book, did you consider that the behaviors you are teaching or modeling to your advisees and junior colleagues could be indicative of incivility, bullying, and workplace aggression?

- As you read this book, did you recognize any administrative behaviors on your campus that support or rebuke incivility, workplace aggression, and bullying?

- Now that you have read the book, will you make an effort to challenge incivility, the bully, or the academic bully culture?

OR

- Now that you have read the book, will you retreat into your silo, ignore victimized colleagues, and thereby allow the academic bully culture to flourish?

This book has investigated several sources that cause and exacerbate incivility and bully behavior through individual upbringing, structural support, cultural norms, diversity, and corporate influence. We have suggested that in an effort to be visionary, mission driven, financially solvent, diverse, and all things to all people, higher education has created a bully. What once stalked the playground may now work in academe.

This book has made it clear that the only way to eliminate, or at least minimize the impact of, the bully is to recognize the behavior and the perpetrator and address it. This effort will have value not only to the individual being bullied but will benefit the entire institution, as well as the academic profession. Eliminating bully behavior should redirect valuable time and energy to what should occur in higher education: excellent research and teaching.

References

Abdennur, A. (2000). *Camouflaged aggression: The hidden threat to individuals and organizations.* Calgary, Alberta: Detselig Enterprises.

Abramson, J. (1975). *The invisible woman.* San Francisco: Jossey-Bass.

Adams, H. (1988). *The academic tribes* (2nd ed.). Urbana: University of Illinois Press.

Altbach, P. (1995). Problems and possibilities: The U.S. academic profession. *Studies in Higher Education, 20,* 27–44.

Altbach, P., & Finkelstein, M. (Eds.). (1997). *The academic profession: The professoriate in crisis.* New York: Garland.

Appleton, J., Briggs, C., Rhatigan, J., & Anderson, C. (Eds.). (1978). *Pieces of eight.* Portland, OR: NASPA Institute for Research and Development.

Aquirre, A., Jr. (2000). *Women and minority faculty in the academic workplace.* Washington, DC: George Washington University Press.

Austin, A., & Gamson, Z. (1983). *Academic culture: New demands heightened tensions.* Washington, DC: George Washington University Press.

Baez, B. (2002). Confidentiality and peer review: The paradox of secrecy in academe. *Review of Higher Education, 25,* 163–183.

Baldridge, J. V. (1971). *Power and conflict in the university.* Hoboken, NJ: Wiley.

Bandura, A. (1973). *Aggression: A social learning analysis.* Upper Saddle River, NJ: Prentice Hall.

Barash, D. (2003). *The survival game: How game theory explains the biology of cooperation and competition.* New York: Holt.

Barash, D. (2004, June 25). Birds do it, bees do it—Should professors, too, strive to communicate sincerity? *Chronicle of Higher Education,* B9–10.

Becher, T., & Trowler, P. (2001). *Academic tribe and territories: Intellectual enquiry and the culture of disciplines* (2nd ed.). Philadelphia: Society for Research in Higher Education and Open University Press.

Becker, H., & Carper, J. (1966). Professional identification. In H. Vollmer & D. Mills (Eds.), *Professionalization* (pp. 101–108). Upper Saddle River, NJ: Prentice Hall.

Benjamin, R., & Carroll, S. (1998). The implications of the changed environment for governance in higher education. In W. Tierney (Ed.), *The responsive university* (pp. 92–119). Baltimore, MD: Johns Hopkins University Press.

Bennett, J. (1998). *College professionalism: The academy, individuation, and the common good.* Phoenix, AZ: Oryx Press.

Bennis, W. (1989). *Why leaders can't lead.* San Francisco: Jossey-Bass.

Bensimon, E. (1990). The new president and understanding the campus as a culture. In W. Tierney (Ed.), *Assessing academic climates and cultures* (pp. 75–86). San Francisco: Jossey-Bass.

Berger, P., & Luckman, T. (1967). *The social construction of reality.* New York: Anchor Books.

Bergquist, W. (1992). *Four cultures of the academy.* San Francisco: Jossey-Bass.

Berkenkotter, C. (1995). The power and perils of peer review. *Rhetoric Review,* 13, 245–248.

Blackburn, R., & Lawrence, J. (1995). Faculty research. In *Faculty at work: Motivation, expectations, satisfaction* (pp. 115–176). Baltimore, MD: Johns Hopkins University Press.

Bland, C., Center, B., Finstad, D., Risbey, K., & Staples, J. (2006). The impact of appointment type on the productivity and commitment of full-time faculty in research and doctoral institutions. *Journal of Higher Education,* 77, 89–123.

Blau, P. (1994). *The organization of academic work* (2nd ed.). New Brunswick, NJ: Transaction.

Bloom, A. (1987). *Closing of the American mind.* Needham Heights, MA: Pearson.

Bode, R. (1996, November). *Collegiality encountered by new faculty.* Paper presented at the annual meeting of the Association for the Study of Higher Education, Memphis, TN.

Bollinger, L. (2005, April 8). The value and responsibilities of academic freedom [Point of View]. *Chronicle of Higher Education,* B20.

Bourdieu, P. (1977). *Outline of a theory practice.* Cambridge: Cambridge University Press.

Bowen, H. (2001). The interpretation of voting in the allocation of economic resources. In J. M. Buchanan (Ed.), *Landmark papers in economics, politics, and law.* Northampton, MA: Edward Elgar.

Boyer, E. (1990). The scholarship of teaching from *Scholarship reconsidered: Priorities of the professoriate. College Teaching, 39*(1), 11–13.

Boyer, E. (1997). *Ernest Boyer: Selected speeches 1979–1995.* Princeton, NJ: Carnegie Foundation for the Advancement of Teaching.

Braithwaite, R. (2001). *Managing aggression.* New York: Routledge.

Braskamp, L., & Wergin, J. (1998). Forming new social partnerships. In W. Tierney (Ed.), *The responsive university* (pp. 78–91). Baltimore, MD: Johns Hopkins University Press.

Braxton, J., & Bayer, A. (1999). *Faculty misconduct in collegiate teaching.* Baltimore, MD: Johns Hopkins University Press.

Brodsky, C. (1976). *The harassed worker.* Lanham, MD: Lexington Books.

Brubaker, J., & Rudy, W. (1997). *Higher education in transition* (4th ed.) New York: HarperCollins.

Burghardt, D., & Colbeck, C. (2005). Women's studies faculty at the intersection of institutional power and feminist values. *Journal of Higher Education, 76,* 301–330.

Caldwell, M. (1999). *A short history of rudeness: Manners, morals, and misbehavior in modern America.* New York: Picador.

Campbell, J. (2000). *Dry rot in the ivory tower.* Lanham, MD: University Press of America.

Carter, S. (1998). *Civility: Manners, morals, and the etiquette of democracy.* New York: Basic Books.

Casbon, J., & Hurtig-Casbon, C. (2005). *Inquiry into organizational wholeness and non-violence.* Unpublished manuscript.

Chesler, P. (1972). *Women and madness.* New York: Avon Books.

Chism, N. (2006). Teaching awards: What do they award? *Journal of Higher Education, 77,* 589–617.

Church, R., & Sedlak, M. (1977). The antebellum college and academy. In L. Goodchild & H. Wechsler (Eds.), *The history of higher education* (pp. 131–148). Needham Heights, MA: Pearson.

Clark, L. (1977). Fact and fantasy: A recent profile of women in academia. *Peabody Journal of Education, 54,* 103–109.

Clark, S., & Corcoran, S. (1986). Perspectives of the professional socialization of women faculty. *Journal of Higher Education, 57,* 20–43.

Cornesky, R., & McCool, S. (1994). *Total Quality Improvement guide for institutions of higher education.* Madison, WI: Magna Publications.

Coyne, I., Craig, J., & Smith-Lee Chong, P. (2004). Workplace bullying in a group context. *British Journal of Guidance and Counseling, 32,* 301–317.

Creamer, E. (2004). Collaborators' attitudes about differences of opinion. *Journal of Higher Education, 75,* 556–571.

Cremin, L. (1970). *American education: The colonial experience, 1607–1783.* New York: HarperCollins.

Dahrendorf, R. (1958). Out of utopia: Toward a reorientation of sociological analysis. *American Journal of Sociology, 64,* 115–127.

Damrosch, D. (1995). *We scholars: Changing the culture of the university.* Cambridge, MA: Harvard University Press.

Davenport, N., Schwartz, R., & Elliott, G. (1999). *Mobbing: Emotional abuse in the American workplace.* Ames, IA: Civil Society Publishing.

Dawn, J., Cowie, H., & Ananiadou, K. (2003). Perceptions and experience of workplace bullying in five different working populations. *Aggressive Behavior, 29,* 489–496.

Deming, W. E. (1986). *Out of the crisis.* Cambridge, MA: Massachusetts Institute of Technology, Center for Advanced Engineering Study.

Dennison, D. (1990). *Corporate culture and organizational effectiveness.* Hoboken, NJ: Wiley.

de Waal, F. (2005, September 23). We're all Machiavellians. *Chronicle of Higher Education,* B10.

Diamond, R. (1993). Changing priorities and the faculty reward system. In R. Diamond & B. Adam (Eds.), *Recognizing faculty work: Reward systems for the year 2000* (pp. 5–22). New Directions for Higher Education, no. 81. San Francisco: Jossey-Bass.

Douglass, M. (1986). *How institutions think.* Syracuse, NY: Syracuse University Press.

D'Souza, D. (1991). *Illiberal education: The politics of race and sex on campus.* New York: Free Press.

Duderstadt, J., & Womack, F. (2003). *The future of the public university in America: Beyond the crossroads.* Baltimore, MD: John Hopkins University Press.

Durkheim, E. (1953). *Sociology and philosophy.* New York: Free Press.

Dziech, B., & Weiner, L. (1990). *The lecherous professor* (2nd ed.) Urbana: University of Illinois Press.

Eagleton, T. (2000). *The idea of culture.* Oxford: Blackwell Publishers.

Einarsen, D. (1999). The nature and causes of bullying at work. *International Journal of Manpower, 20,* 16–27.

Etaugh, C. (1984). Women faculty and administrators in higher education: Changes in their status since 1972. *Journal of the National Association of Women Deans, Advisors, and Counselors, 48*(1), 21–25.

Fairweather, J. (2002). The ultimate faculty evaluation: Promotion and tenure decisions. In C. Colbeck (Ed.), *Evaluating faculty performance* (pp. 97–109). New Directions for Institutional Research, no. 114. San Francisco: Jossey-Bass.

Farley, J. (1985). Women versus academe: Who's winning? *Journal of Social Issues, 41*(4), 111–120.

Ferris, P. (2004). A personal view: A preliminary typology of organizational response to allegations of workplace bullying: See no evil, hear no evil, speak no evil. *British Journal of Guidance Counseling, 32,* 389–395.

Ferriss, A. (2002). Studying and measuring civility: A framework, trends, and scale. *Sociological Inquiry, 72,* 376–392.

Festinger, L. (1954). A theory of social comparison process. *Human Relations, 7,* 117–140.

Finkelstein, M. (1997). From tutor to specialized scholar: Academic professionalization in eighteenth and nineteenth century America. In L. Goodchild & H. Wechsler (Eds.), *The history of higher education* (pp. 80–93). Needham Heights, MA: Simon & Schuster.

Finkelstein, M., Seal, R., & Schuster, J. (1998). *The new academic generation: A profession in transformation.* Baltimore, MD: Johns Hopkins University Press.

Fogg, P. (2003, March 21). Academic therapists: Hoping to avoid lawsuits and rancor, more colleges use conflict-resolution experts. *Chronicle of Higher Education,* A12–13.

Franke, A. (2005, June 25). Personal antagonisms: When employees charge retaliation. *Chronicle of Higher Education,* B14–16.

Freeland, R. (1997). The world transformed: A golden age for American universities, 1945–1970. In L. Goodchild & H. Wechsler (Eds.), *The history of higher education* (pp. 587–609). Needham Heights, MA: Pearson.

French, J.P.R., & Raven, R. (1960). The bases of social power. In D. Cartwright & A. Zander (eds.), *Group dynamics* (pp. 607–623). New York: Harper-Collins.

Gamson, Z. (1997). Higher education and rebuilding civic life. *Change, 29*(1), 10–13.

Gayle, D. J., Bhoendradatt, T., & White, A. Q. (2003). *Governance in the twenty-first century university: Approaches to effective leadership and management.* San Francisco: Jossey-Bass.

Giebel, D. (2005). When professors cheat. In K. Westhues (Ed.), *Winning, losing, moving on: How professionals deal with workplace harassment and mobbing* (pp. 75–121). Lewiston, NY: Edwin Mellen Press.

Glazer-Raymo, J. (1999). *Shattering the myth: Women in academe.* Baltimore, MD: Johns Hopkins University Press.

Goffman, E. (1959). *The presentation of self in everyday life.* New York: Doubleday.

Goffman, E. (1963). *Behavior in public places.* New York: Free Press.

Goffman, E. (1967). *Interaction ritual.* New York: Doubleday.

Goffman, E. (1974). *Frame analysis.* New York: HarperCollins.

Goldberg, S. (1973). *The inevitability of patriarchy.* New York: Morrow.

Golde, C. (2005). The role of the department and discipline in doctoral student attrition: Lessons from four departments. *Journal of Higher Education, 76,* 669–700.

Gordon, L. (1997). From seminary to university: An overview of women's higher education, 1987–1920. In L. Goodchild & H. Wechsler (Eds.), *The history of higher education* (p. 473–498). Needham Heights, MA: Pearson.

Gould, E. (2003). *The university as a corporate culture.* New Haven, CT: Yale University Press.

Gouldner, A. (1957). Cosmopolitans and locals: Toward an analysis of latent social roles. *Administrative Science Quarterly, 2,* 281–305.

Gouldner, A. (1958). Cosmopolitans and locals: Toward an analysis of latent social roles I. *Administrative Science Quarterly, 2,* 444–480.

Greenleaf, R. (1970). *The servant as leader.* Cambridge, MA: Center for Applied Studies.

Grubb, W. N., & Lazerson, M. (2005). Vocationalism in higher education: The triumph of the education gospel. *Journal of Higher Education, 76,* 1–25.

Gruber, C. (1997). Backdrop. In L. Goodchild & H. Wechsler (Eds.), *The history of higher education* (pp. 203–221). Needham Heights, MA: Pearson.

Guiffrida, D. (2006). Toward a cultural advancement of Tinto's theory. *Review of Higher Education, 29,* 451–472.

Haag, P. (2005, February 11). Navigating the new subtleties of sex-discrimination cases in academe [Point of View]. *Chronicle of Higher Education,* B20.

Hadikin, R., & O'Driscoll, M. (2000). *The bullying culture: Cause, effect, harm reduction.* Oxford: Butterworth-Heinemann.

Hannabus, S. (1998). Bullying at work. *Library Management, 19,* 304–310.

Hart, J. (2006). Women and feminism in higher education scholarship: An analysis of three core journals. *Journal of Higher Education, 77,* 40–61.

Heim, P., & Murphy, S. (2001). *In the company of women.* New York: Jeremy P. Tarcher/Putnam.

Helgesen, S. (1995). *The web of inclusion: A new architecture for building great organizations.* New York: Doubleday.

Henry, S. (2004). Bullying—Like father like son? The contentious findings of a year long study. *Education Journal, 76*, 23–26.

Herbst, J. (1976). From religion to politics: Debates and confrontations over American colonial governance in mid-eighteenth century America. *Harvard Educational Review, 46*, 397–424.

Hermanowicz, J. (2005). Classifying universities and their departments: A social world perspective. *Journal of Higher Education, 76*, 26–55.

Hershberg, J. (1993). *James B. Conant: Harvard to Hiroshima and the making of the nuclear age.* New York: Knopf.

Herzberg, F., Mausner, B., & Snyderman, B. B. (1959). *The motivation to work.* Hoboken, NJ: Wiley.

Hoel, H., Einarsen, S., & Cooper, C. (2003). Organizational effects of bullying. In S. Einarsen, H. Hoel, D. Zapf, & C. Cooper (Eds.), *Bullying and emotional abuse in the workplace: International perspectives in research and practice* (pp. 145–161). London: Taylor and Francis.

Hoel, H., Faragher, B., & Cooper, C. (2004). Bullying is detrimental to health, but all bullying behaviours are not necessarily equally damaging. *British Journal of Guidance and Counseling, 32*, 367–387.

Hoel, H., & Salin, D. (2003). Organizational antecedents of workplace bullying. In S. Einarsen, H. Hoel, D. Zapf, & C. Cooper (Eds.), Bullying and emotional abuse in the workplace: International perspectives in research and practice (pp. 203–218). London: Taylor and Francis.

Hollon, C., & Gemmill, G. (1976). A comparison of female and male professors on participation in decision-making, job related tension, involvement, and job satisfaction. *Educational Administration Quarterly, 12*, 80–93.

Hood, C. (1994). *Explaining economic policy reversals.* Bristol, PA: Open University Press.

Horine, J., Hailey, W., & Rubach, L. (1993). Shaping America's future. *Quality Progress, 26*(10), 41–51.

Huber, M. (2002). Faculty evaluation and the development of academic careers. In C. Colbeck (Eds.), *Evaluating faculty performance* (pp. 73–83). New Directions for Institutional Advancement, no. 114. San Francisco: Jossey-Bass.

Hume, K. (2003, January 31). Department politics as a foreign language. *Chronicle of Higher Education*, B5.

Huston, T., Norman, M., & Ambrose, S. (2007). Expanding the discussion of faculty vitality to include productive but disengaged senior faculty. *Journal of Higher Education, 78*, 493–522.

Hutcheson, P. (1997). McCarthyism and the professoriate: A historiographic nightmare? In L. Goodchild & H. Wechsler (Eds.), *The history of higher education* (pp. 610–627). Needham Heights, MA: Pearson.

Ironside, M., & Seifert, R. (2003). Tackling bullying in the workplace: The collective dimension. In S. Einarsen, H. Hoel, D. Zapf, & C. Cooper (Eds.), *Bullying and emotional abuse in the workplace: International perspectives in research and practice* (pp. 383–398). London: Taylor and Francis.

Janis, I. (1982). Groupthink: Psychological studies of policy decisions and fiascoes (2nd ed.). Boston: Houghton Mifflin.

Janis, I. (1988). Groupthink. In R. Katz (Ed.), *Managing professionals in innovative organizations: A collection of readings* (pp. 332–340). New York: HarperCollins.

Jennifer, D., Cowie, H., & Ananiadou, K. (2003). Perceptions and experience of workplace bullying in five different working populations. *Aggressive Behavior, 29,* 489–496.

Julius, D., Baldridge, V., & Pfeffer, J. (1999). A memo from Machiavelli. *Journal of Higher Education, 70,* 113–129.

Kanter, R. (1977). *Men and women of the corporation.* New York: Basic Books.

Kanungo, R. (1982). *Work alienation: An integrative approach.* New York: Praeger.

Kaplin, W., & Lee, B. (1995). *The law of higher education* (3rd ed.). San Francisco: Jossey-Bass.

Katz, S. (2006, October 6). What has happened to the professoriate? *Chronicle of Higher Education,* B8–11.

Keashly, L., & Jagatic, K. (2003). American perspectives on workplace bullying. In S. Einarsen, H. Hoel, D. Zapf, & C. Cooper (Eds.), *Bullying and emotional abuse in the workplace: International perspectives in research and practice* (pp. 31–61). London: Taylor and Francis.

Kelley, M., & Parsons, B. (2000). Sexual harassment in the 1990s: A universitywide survey of female faculty, administrators, staff, and students. *Journal of Higher Education, 71,* 548–566.

Kember, D. (1998). Action research: Towards an alternative framework for educational development. *Distance Education, 19*(1), 43–63.

Kerr, C. (1982). *The uses of the university.* Cambridge, MA: Harvard University Press.

Kezar, A. (2000). Pluralistic leadership: Incorporating diverse voices. *Journal of Higher Education, 71,* 722–743.

Kezar, A. (2005). Consequences of radical change in governance: A grounded theory approach. *Journal of Higher Education, 76,* 634–668.

Klein, R. (2005). You can't turn someone down for promotion because you don't like him. In K. Westhues (Ed.), *Winning, losing, moving on: How professionals deal with workplace harassment and mobbing* (pp. 53–74). Lewiston, NY: Edwin Mellen Press.

Lane, A. (2005, May 5). Gender, power, and sexuality: First, do no harm. *Chronicle of Higher Education*, B10, B12–13.

Lang, J. (2005). *Life on the tenure track*. Baltimore, MD: Johns Hopkins University Press.

Lee, B. (2004, June 25). Colleges should plan now for a financial crunch. *Chronicle of Higher Education*, B8–9.

Legislative Office of Education Oversight. (1993). *The faculty reward system in public universities*. Columbus, OH: Author.

Lenzner, R., & Johnson, S. (1997, March 10). Peter Drucker—Seeing things as they really are. *Forbes Magazine Online*. Retrieved August 20, 2007, from http://www.forbes.com?forbes/97/0310/5905122a.htm.

Lévi-Strauss, C. (1963). *Structural anthropology*. New York: Basic Books.

Levin, J. (2006). Faculty work: Tensions between educational and economic values. *Journal of Higher Education, 77*, 62–88.

Lewis, D. (2004). Bullying at work: The impact of shame among university and college lecturers. *British Journal of Guidance and Counseling, 32*, 281–299.

Lewis, D., & Rayner, C. (2003). Bullying and human resource management: A wolf in sheep's clothing? In S. Einarsen, H. Hoel, D. Zapf, & C. Cooper (Eds.), *Bullying and emotional abuse in the workplace: International perspectives in research and practice* (pp. 370–382). London: Taylor and Francis.

Life application Bible study: James. (1998). Wheaton, IL: Tyndale House.

Lindholm, J. (2004). Pathways to the professoriate: The role of self, others, and environment in shaping academic career aspirations. *Journal of Higher Education, 75*, 603–635.

Lomperis, A. (1990). Are women changing the nature of the academic profession? *Journal of Higher Education, 61*, 643–677.

Lynton, E. (1995). *Making the case for professional service*. Washington, DC: American Association for Higher Education.

Mallard, K. (2002). The soul of scholarship. In K. Zahorski (Eds.), *Scholarship in the postmodern era: New venues, new values, new visions* (pp. 59–69). New Directions for Teaching and Learning, no. 90. San Francisco: Jossey-Bass.

Market forces, leadership, and the future of higher education. (n.d.). In *Research annals: A publication of the Program in Higher, Adult, and Lifelong Education.* East Lansing: Michigan State University.

Maslow, A. (1949). Our maligned animal nature. *Journal of Psychology, 28,* 273–278.

McCarthy, P. (2003). Bullying at work: A postmodern experience. In S. Einarsen, H. Hoel, D. Zapf, & C. Cooper (Eds.), *Bullying and emotional abuse in the workplace: International perspectives in research and practice* (pp. 231–244). London: Taylor and Francis.

McCarthy, P., & Mayhew, C. (2004). *Safeguarding the organization against violence and bullying: An international perspective.* New York: Palgrave Macmillan.

McGinnis, R., & Long, J. S. (1988). Entry into academic: Effects of stratification, geography, and ecology. In D. Breneman & T. Youn (Eds.), *Academic labor markets and careers* (pp. 28–51). Philadelphia: Falmer Press.

Mead, G. H. (1934). *Mind, self, and society: From the standpoint of a social behaviorist.* Chicago: University of Chicago Press.

Menges, R. J., & Weimer, M. (1996). *Teaching on solid ground: Using scholarship to improve practice.* San Francisco: Jossey-Bass.

Merton, R. K. (1949). *Social theory and social structure.* New York: Free Press.

Milgram, S. (1963). Behavioral study of obedience. *Journal of Abnormal and Social Psychology, 67,* 371–378.

Miller, J. B. (1986). *Toward a new psychology of women* (2nd ed). Boston: Beacon Press.

Miller, J. B. (1995). Domination/subordination. In J. T. Wren (Ed.), *Leader's companion* (pp. 222–230). New York: Free Press.

Minor, J. (2004). Understanding faculty senates: Moving from mystery to models. *Review of Higher Education, 27,* 343–364.

Montagu, A. (1956). *The biosocial nature of man.* New York: Grove Press.

Montez, J., Wolverton, M., & Gmelch, W. (2002). The roles and challenges of deans. *Review of Higher Education, 26,* 241–266.

Montgomery, K., Kane, K., & Vance, C. (2004). Accounting for differences in norms of respect: A study of assessments of incivility through the lenses of race and gender. *Group and Organizational Management, 29,* 248–268.

Morphew, C., & Hartley, M. (2006). Mission statements: A thematic analysis of rhetoric across institutional types. *Journal of Higher Education, 77,* 456–471.

Morrison, A., & von Glinow, M. A. (1990). Women and minorities in management. *American Psychologist, 45,* 200–208.

Murphy, J. (1999). New consumerism: Evolving market dynamics I: The institutional dimension of schooling. In J. Murphy & K. S. Lewis (Eds.), *Handbook of research on educational administration: A project of the American Educational Research Association* (2nd ed.) San Francisco: Jossey-Bass.

Namie, G., & Namie, R. (2003). *The bully at work.* Naperville, IL: Sourcebooks.

Neilson, G., Pasternak, B., & Van Nuys, K. (2005). The passive-aggressive organization. *Harvard Business Review, 83*(10), 82–92.

Neuman, J., & Baron, R. (2003). Social antecedents of bullying. In S. Einarsen, H. Hoel, D. Zapf, & C. Cooper (Eds.), *Bullying and emotional abuse in the workplace: International perspectives in research and practice* (pp. 185–202). London: Taylor and Francis.

Newman, F., Couturier, L., & Scurry, J. (2004). *The future of higher education: Rhetoric, reality, and the risks of the market.* San Francisco: Jossey-Bass.

Nidiffer, J. (2001). New leadership for a new century. In J. Nidiffer & C. Bashaw (Eds.), *Women administrators in higher education* (pp. 101–134). Albany, NY: SUNY Press.

Ogren, C. (1997). Where coeds were co-educated: Normal school in Wisconsin, 1870–1920. In L. Goodchild & H. Wechsler (Eds.), *The history of higher education* (pp. 347–361). Needham Heights, MA: Pearson.

Olafsson, R. F., & Johannsdottir, H. L. (2004). Coping with bullying in the workplace: The effect of gender, age and type of bullying. *British Journal of Guidance and Counseling, 32,* 319–333.

Owen, P., & Demb, A. (2004). Change dynamics and leadership in technology implementation. *Journal of Higher Education, 75,* 636–666.

Palmieri, P. (1997). From Republican motherhood to race suicide: Argumentation on the higher education of women in the United States, 1820–1920. In L. Goodchild & H. Wechsler (Eds.), *The history of higher education* (pp. 173–182). Needham Heights, MA: Pearson.

Parsons, T., & Platt, G. (1970). Age, social structure, and socialization in higher education. *Sociology of Education, 43,* 1–37.

Paulsen, M., & Feldman, K. (1995). Toward a reconceptualization of scholarship. *Journal of Higher Education, 66,* 615–640.

Peck, D. (2002). Civility: A contemporary context for a meaningful historical concept. *Sociological Inquiry, 72,* 358–375.

Perkin, H. (1997). History of universities. In L. Goodchild & H. Wechsler (Eds.), *The history of higher education* (pp. 3–34). Needham Heights, MA: Pearson.

Perkins, L. (1997). The impact of the "culture of true womanhood" on the education of black women. In L. Goodchild & H. Wechsler (Eds.), *The history of higher education* (pp. 183–190). Needham Heights, MA: Pearson.

Peyton, P. R. (2003). *Dignity at work: Eliminate bullying and create a positive working environment.* Hove, UK: Brunner-Routledge.

Phillips, T., & Smith, P. (2003). Everyday incivility: Towards a benchmark. *Sociological Review, 51,* 85–108.

Potts, D. (1997). "College enthusiasm!" as public response: 1800–1860. In L. Goodchild & H. Wechsler (Eds.), *The history of higher education* (pp. 149–161). Needham Heights, MA: Pearson.

Powers, J. (2003). Commercializing academic research. *Journal of Higher Education, 74,* 26–50.

Pressing legal issues: 10 views of the next 5 years. (2004, June 25). *Chronicle of Higher Education,* B4–7.

Putnam, R. (2000). *Bowling alone: The collapse and revival of American community.* New York: Simon & Schuster.

Rayner, C., Hoel, H., & Cooper, C. L. (2002). *Workplace bullying: What we know, who is to blame, and what can we do?* London: Taylor and Francis.

Readings, B. (1996). *The university in ruins.* Cambridge, MA: Harvard University Press.

Reynolds, A. (1992). Charting the changes in junior faculty. *Journal of Higher Education, 63,* 639–652.

Richards, J., & Daley, H. (2003). Bullying policy: Development, implementation, and monitoring. In S. Einarsen, H. Hoel, D. Zapf, & C. Cooper (Eds.), *Bullying and emotional abuse in the workplace: International perspectives in research and practice* (pp. 247–258). London: Taylor and Francis.

Robbins, L., & Kahn, E. (1985). Sex discrimination and sex equity for faculty women in the 1980s. *Journal of Social Issues, 41*(4), 1–16.

Rosenzweig, R. (1998). *The political university: Policy, politics, ad presidential leadership in American research universities.* Baltimore, MD: Johns Hopkins University Press.

Rosser, V., Johnsrud, L., & Heck, R. (2003). Academic deans and directors: Assessing their effectiveness from individual and institutional perspectives. *Journal of Higher Education, 74,* 1–25.

Rossides, D. (2004). Knee jerk formalism: Reforming American education. *Journal of Higher Education, 75,* 667–703.

Ruger, P., & Bickel, R. (2004, June 25). The ubiquitous college lawyer. *Chronicle of Higher Education*, B1–4.

Said, E. (1993). *Culture and imperialism*. New York: Knopf.

Salin, D. (2003). Ways of explaining workplace bullying: A review of enabling, motivating, and precipitating structure and processes in the work environment. *Human Relations, 56*, 1213–1232.

Schein, E. (1992). *Organizational culture and leadership* (2nd ed.). San Francisco: Jossey-Bass.

Schlossberg, N. (1974). The right to be wrong is gone: Women in academe. *Educational Record, 55*, 257–262.

Schuster, J., and Associates. (1994). *Strategic governance: How to make big decisions better*. Phoenix, AZ: Oryx Press.

Schuster, J., & Finkelstein, M. (2006). *The American faculty: The restructuring of academic work and careers*. Baltimore, MD: Johns Hopkins University Press.

Scott, J. (2006). The mission of the university: Medieval to postmodern transformation. *Journal of Higher Education, 77*, 1–39.

Seldin, P. (1984). *Changing practices in faculty evaluation*. San Francisco: Jossey-Bass.

Senge, P. (1990). *The fifth discipline*. New York: Doubleday.

Sennett, R. (1976). *The fall of public man: On the social psychology of capitalism*. New York: Vintage Books.

Settles, I., Cortina, L., Malley, J., & Stewart, A. (2006). The climate for women in academic science: The good, the bad, and the changeable. *Psychology of Women Quarterly, 30*, 47–58.

Shavlik, D., & Touchton, J. (1984). Toward a new era of leadership: The National Identification Program. In A. Tinsley, C. Secor, & S. Kaplan (Eds.), *Women in higher education* (pp. 47–58). New Directions for Higher Education, no. 45. San Francisco: Jossey-Bass.

Sheehan, M., & Jordan, P. (2003). Bullying, emotions, and the learning organization. In S. Einarsen, H. Hoel, D. Zapf, & C. Cooper (Eds.), *Bullying and emotional abuse in the workplace: International perspectives in research and practice* (pp. 359–369). London: Taylor and Francis.

Shelley, P. (2004, June 25). Colleges need to give students intensive care. *Chronicle of Higher Education*, B16.

Skinner, B. F. (1953). *Science and human behavior*. New York: Macmillan.

Slaughter, S., Archerd, C., & Campbell, T. (2004). Boundaries and quandaries: How professors negotiate market relations. *Review of Higher Education, 28*, 129–165.

Slawski, C. (1973, August). *Personal socialization in organizational context: Hypotheses and comparative cases.* Paper presented at the annual meeting of the America Psychological Association, New York. [ERIC Document Reproduction Service No. ED 157 451]

Smart, J., & St. John, E. (1996). Organizational culture and effectiveness in higher education: A test of the "culture type" and "strong culture" hypothesis. *Educational Evaluation and Policy Analysis, 18,* 219–241.

Smith, P. K., Singer, M., Hoel, H., & Cooper, C. L. (2003). Victimization in the school and the workplace: Are there any links? *British Journal of Psychology, 94,* 175–188.

Solomon, B. (1989). Demographic changes and women on campus. *American Behavioral Scientist, 32,* 640–646.

Sorcinelli, M. A. (2002). New conceptions of scholarship for a new generation of faculty members. In K. Zahorski (Ed.), *Scholarship in the post-modern era: New venues, new values, new visions* (pp. 41–48). New Directions for Teaching and Learning, no. 90. San Francisco: Jossey-Bass.

Spears, L. (1994). Servant leadership: Toward a new era of caring. In J. Renesch (Ed.), *Leadership in a new era: Visionary approaches to the biggest approaches to the biggest crisis of our time* (pp. 153–166). San Francisco: New Leaders Press.

Sumner, W. G. (1918/1969). *The forgotten man: And other essays.* New Haven, CT: Yale University Press.

Thomas, W. I. (1923). *The unadjusted girl.* New York: Social Science Research Council.

Thompson, G., & Louque, A. (2005). *Exposing the "culture of arrogance" in the academy.* Sterling, VA: Stylus.

Tierney, W. (1997). Organizational socialization in higher education. *Journal of Higher Education, 68,* 1–16.

Tierney, W. (2004). Academic freedom and tenure: Between fiction and reality. *Journal of Research in Higher Education, 75,* 161–177.

Tierney, W., & Bensimon, E. (1996). *Community and socialization in academe.* Albany, NY: SUNY Press.

Trower, C., Austin, A., & Sorcinelli, M. A. (2001, May). Paradise lost: How the academy converts enthusiastic recruits into early career doubters. *AAHE Bulletin, 53*(9), 3–6.

Truss, L. (2005). *Talk to the hand.* New York: Gotham Books.

Twale, D., & Lane, T. (2006, February). *Faculty performance measures: Cultural and social effects of workload, merit, tenure and promotion policy alignment.*

Paper presented at the annual meeting of the Eastern Educational Research Association, Hilton Head, SC.

Twale, D., & Shannon, D. (1996). Gender differences among faculty in campus governance: Nature of involvement, satisfaction, and power. *Initiatives, 57*(4), 11–19.

Van Alstyne, W. (1997). Tenure: A summary, explanation, and defense. *AAUP Bulletin, 57*, 328–333.

Veysey, L. (1965). *The emergence of the American university.* Chicago: University of Chicago Press.

Vollmer, H., & Mills, D. (Eds.). (1966). *Professionalization.* Upper Saddle River, NJ: Prentice Hall.

von Herder, J. G. (2000). *Ideas on the philosophy of history of humankind.* In R. Bernasconi & T. Lott (Eds.), *The idea of race.* Indianapolis, IN: Hacket Publishing.

Washburn, J. (2005). *University Inc.: The corporate corruption of higher education.* New York: Basic Books.

Weber, M. (1948). The nation. In H. Gerth & C. W. Mills (Trans.) and L. Goodchild & H. Wechsler (Eds.), *The history of higher education* (pp. 571–586). Needham Heights, MA: Pearson.

Wechsler, H. (1997). In academic Gresham's Law: Group repulsion as a theme in American higher education. In L. Goodchild & H. Wechsler (Eds.), *The history of higher education* (pp. 416–431). Needham Heights, MA: Pearson.

Weick, K. (1976). Educational organizations as loosely coupled systems. *Administrative Science Quarterly, 21*, 1–19.

Weidman, J., Twale, D., & Stein, E. (2001). *Socialization of graduate and professional students in higher education: A perilous passage?* San Francisco: Jossey-Bass.

Weiner, D. (2002). *Power freaks: Dealing with them in the workplace or anyplace.* New York: Prometheus Books.

Westhues, K. (2005). *Winning, losing, moving on: How professionals deal with workplace harassment and mobbing.* Lewiston, NY: Edwin Mellen Press.

White, S. (2004). A psychodynamic perspective of workplace bullying: Containment, boundaries and a futile search for recognition. *British Journal of Guidance and Counseling, 32*, 269–280.

Williams, R. (1976). *Keywords.* London: Fontana.

Winston, G. (1997). Why can't a college be more like a firm? *Change, 5*, 33–38.

Winston, G. (1999). Subsidies, hierarchy, and peers. *Journal of Economic Perspectives, 13*, 13–36.

Wright, B. (1997). For the children of the infidels? American Indian education in the colonial colleges. In L. Goodchild & H. Wechsler (Eds.), *The history of higher education* (pp. 72–79). Needham Heights, MA: Pearson.

Wright, M. (2005). Always at odds? Congruence in faculty beliefs about teaching at a research university. *Journal of Higher Education, 76,* 331–353.

Yoder, J. (1985). An academic woman as a token: A case study. *Journal of Social Issues, 41*(4), 61–72.

Young, M. (1978). Sex discrimination in higher education. *Civil Liberties Review, 5*(4), 41–43.

Young, R. (1995). *Colonial desire: Hybridity in theory, culture, and race.* New York: Routledge.

Zapf, D., & Einarsen, S. (2003). Individual antecedents of bullying: Victims and perpetrators. In S. Einarsen, H. Hoel, D. Zapf, & C. L. Cooper (Eds.), *Bullying and emotional abuse in the workplace: International perspectives in research and practice* (pp. 165–184). London: Taylor and Francis.

Zemsky, R., Wegner, G., & Massy, W. (2005). *Remaking the American university.* New Brunswick, NJ: Rutgers University Press.

Name Index

Subject Index

A

Academia. *See* higher education

Academic citizenship, and power, 164–166

Academic culture: and academic freedom, 102; change in, 100–101; collegiality in, 102–105; defined, 98; henhouse analogy for, 127–130; inequity promoted by, 116–118; and intellectual climate, 101–102, 107; and social knowledge of faculty, 106–107; socialization into, 98–99, 109–110. *See also* bully culture; corporate culture

Academic departments: and faculty selection, 71; incivility in, 10–11; socialization vs. acculturation in, 55

Academic freedom: and academic culture, 102; vs. paternalism, 44–45

Action research, 170

Administration: faculty vs., 39–40, 86–90, 135–136, 138, 141–142, 144–145; role of, in bully culture, 176; unaware of bullying, 64. *See also* leadership

African Americans, 36–37, 38, 124–125

Aggression: camouflaged, as means of social control, 104–105; causes of, 13; concealed, 51–52; defined, 13, 48; as foundation of modern

university, 44; gender differences in, 52–54, 61–62; increased with systemic change, 111; and management styles, 62–64; as socially learned, 47–50, 54–55; supported by organizational governance structure, 79–81; workplace behaviors defined as, 13–14. *See also* workplace harassment

Alienation, 44

American Association of University Professors (AAUP), 44, 185

B

Bayh-Dole Act (1980), 42

Bowling Alone (Putnam), 3

Brown v. Topeka Board of Education, 38

Bullies: characteristics of, 22; and leadership, 22–23; power of, 57–62; rehabilitating, 181

Bully culture: acceptance of, 149; administration's role in, 176; assessing, in workplace, 190; deconstructing to change, 181–183; gathering and analyzing data on, 169–175; halting behaviors of, 155; and sexual harassment policies, 152–154, 178; training and education to avoid, 155–162; warning signs of, 150–152. *See also* workplace harassment